CLEM SUNTER

The World and South Africa in the 1990s

HUMAN & ROUSSEAU
TAFELBERG

First published in 1987 jointly by
Human & Rousseau (Pty) Ltd, State House, 3-9 Rose Street, Cape Town;
and Tafelberg Publishers Ltd, 28 Wale Street, Cape Town
Set in 10,5 on 13 pt Plantin by Diatype Setting, Cape Town
Printed and bound by National Book Printers, Goodwood, Cape
First edition, ninth impression 1990

ISBN 0 7981 2177 7

TO MARGARET,
KATY, ROBERT
AND DAVID

Contents

Acknowledgements

This book is based on research undertaken by overseas and South African teams commissioned by Anglo American Corporation of South Africa to look at scenarios for the 1990s. In the overseas team, I especially want to thank Pierre Wack and Ted Newland (both formerly of Royal Dutch Shell), who made an immense contribution to the exercise. Other consultants whose contribution was significant were Edouard Parker, Hughes de Jouvenel, Michael Kaser, Henry Ergas and PA Technology. Parts of the original research for the global material and the entire consolidation of the global exercise were the responsibility of Charter Consolidated's Research and Economic Services Department in London. In this regard I would like to thank Luc Smets, Allan Newey, Yugo Kovach, Jackie Steinitz, Paul Missen and Ian Emsley. Since the completion of the project in 1985, I have taken the opportunity to read a wide variety of literature on global trends, some of which has influenced the putting together of the talk and the book, and provided statistical support to the conclusions of our teams. It would be impossible to acknowledge all the sources, but one book I would single out is *Strategy in the Use of Intellectual Property* by Derek Momberg and Arthur Ashton which deals very comprehensively with the whole issue of transfer of knowledge between countries.

For the South African material, I would like to thank Michael O'Dowd, Bobby Godsell, Michael Spicer and Jim Buys, all of whom are colleagues of mine at Anglo. I would point out that whilst the talk is almost entirely based on their research some of the conclusions expressed in the second part of the book are my own, not theirs. One other valuable source of information is the Institute for Futures Research of the University of Stellenbosch which is producing some of the most important scenario work taking place in South Africa at the moment.

For the assistance in helping me to coordinate the scenario project and put the book together, I would especially like to thank Michael

O'Connor. Without him, this talk would never have been put into hard copy. For secretarial services I thank Gill Brown, Grace Sutherland and Muriel Cromey-Hawke, and for the translation into Afrikaans, Julia Viljoen.

I would like to express my appreciation to Anglo for giving me support throughout this project and for giving me total discretion over the material. In that sense, the views expressed in this book are the teams' and my own – they do not reflect a 'corporate viewpoint'.

Lastly, I would like to thank all the audiences I have had the pleasure of addressing around South Africa, and the organisers of the functions. My schedule was completely handled through word of mouth – 230 audiences comprising 25 000 to 30 000 people from all walks of life. The very access that this talk has had speaks volumes for this country and holds hope for the future. There is a streak of humility here which does not exist elsewhere – people are searching for a solution. South Africa will not be the frog at the bottom of the saucepan of gently heating up water which died because it could not detect the change in temperature! Most people here are aware that the environment is changing. I hope this book gives a little back of the insights I have gained through doing the talk.

Introduction

This short book is the text of a talk which was originally prepared for Anglo American Corporation of South Africa and its associate companies. In July 1986, we decided to make the material available on request to a wider audience in South Africa. The response to such private briefings has been so positive that a further decision was taken to publish the contents. It is a simple talk taking the listener or reader around the world and South Africa in ninety minutes. It does not pretend to be a comprehensive presentation. If we had included all the material that had been obtained over the last three years, the talk would probably have taken a day to deliver. So we have only selected the highlights of all the research that we have done. It is more effective, in any case, to leave certain things unsaid so that people can come to their own conclusions.

No analysis can capture the true complexity of the world or South Africa. However, we hope that the book will provide an effective framework within which people can ask themselves the right questions, debate the future with one another and act on their judgement. Coming from a business environment, I am inevitably trying to weigh the issues of the future from a businessman's point of view. Indeed, that was the original purpose of the talk for Anglo. Yet in spite of this focus, it does seem to have appealed to a very wide spectrum of audiences around South Africa. The talk does not offer specific solutions to South Africa's problems and some people have gone away frustrated by the fact that it ends on a note of possibilities, not certainties. But the very process that we advocate to sort out the problems here precludes one from offering solutions in advance. Let the main actors evolve them along the lines suggested here.

FORECASTS AND SCENARIOS

'I am not going to give a long-term forecast either on the world or South Africa. There are three reasons why we no longer like long-term forecasts:

Firstly, they very seldom come true. The classic example I have is a misjudgement about Japan made by a leading Western expert a few years after the Second World War. He said, "The economic situation in Japan may be fundamentally so unsound that no policies, no matter how wise, can save her from slow economic starvation." At the time, Japan's industrial production was barely 40 per cent of that of the UK. Now it is five times as large. One has to return to the 1950s and 1960s to find a period when forecasting was even remotely successful. In those days the future resembled the past. For the world generally, inflation ran at 2 per cent a year, growth was 5 per cent and the gold price was flat. It was a marvellously mechanistic world. All you had to do was take a past trend and extrapolate it into the future and it came true. But there is no earthly reason why the future should resemble the past. If one goes further back in history, one realises that the 1950s and 1960s were a period of unusual stability. In most decades, major events have happened which no study of the past could have led one to prophesy. One would have had to take an imaginative leap into the future in order to grasp what was going to happen. A quote I was given some time ago summed it up perfectly: "The future is normally not what it used to be."

The 1970s and 1980s so far have certainly been like that − take the two oil price shocks in the 1970s and the erratic behaviour of the price recently. Hence many people's confidence in their powers of prophecy has been rudely shattered. They have come to know that the future is inherently uncertain. Even consensus on the future is dangerous. An employee in a major oil company once said, "In our company it is much better to be wrong than different." To avoid this tendency it is necessary to look at the universe of possibilities.

The second reason why we dislike long-term forecasts is that it is difficult to communicate bad news in a forecast. People do not like being told that something bad is going to happen to them. They blank out. It is preferable to put forward the *possibility* of bad news and offer them a way out. Then it sticks. Predictions of good news abound in business where smoothly rising product price forecasts yield satisfactory earnings projections. Hardly ever do the curves fall. You know deep down, though, that the answer (a satisfactory one to management) is driving the forecast rather than the other way round.

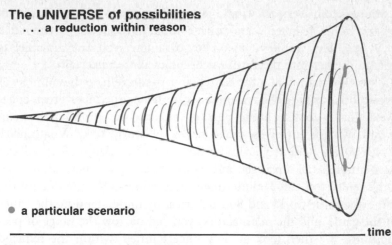

The UNIVERSE of possibilities
. . . a reduction within reason

● **a particular scenario**

time

Chart 1 · The Universe of Possibilities

Lastly, the strongest objection to giving forecasts in the context of South Africa is that one is implying that the future is decided irrespective of any effort on the listeners' or readers' part. Here the future is finely balanced and each and every South African can play a role in influencing it. There are two kinds of future: the 'active future' which you make happen, and the 'passive future' which you let happen to you. The South African material in this book is all about the 'active future', because it is only if people act to make a successful future happen that it will. As you will see, 'scenario planning' encourages people to choose between options. Once they have chosen, it is left to them to formulate the strategies that will fulfil their preferred future.

Faced with the shortcomings of forecasts, Anglo decided to look for a different technique for understanding the future. We were very fortunate in November 1982 to be given a presentation on scenario planning by the then head of the business environment planning unit at Royal Dutch Shell. Shell had developed the system over ten years. We decided to introduce this new approach in Anglo, with the help of several outside consultants.

How does scenario planning work? In Chart 1 you will see a 'Cone of Uncertainty' opening up into the future. For example, if I took a poll among readers on what the gold price was going to be next week,

13

I would get answers covering a range of, say, $30. If I asked readers what it would be in ten years' time, I would have answers over a range of $1 000. This would occur on any parameter you care to name: as you go further into the future it becomes more uncertain.

Now the first job of a scenario planner is to reduce the number of possibilities as far as he reasonably can; hence the inner green cone. We do that by looking at the 'rules of the game' and profiling the main actors. We ask ourselves: what makes the world tick? What makes South Africa tick? If you know the rules of cricket or football and have studied the strengths and weaknesses of the best players on either side, you can exclude many possibilities. We say exactly the same about the world and South Africa; by understanding the 'rules of the game' and the main actors, you can narrow the range of possibilities. We then look at 'key uncertainties' within the reduced cone. These are factors that are incredibly important for the future, but whose movement no one can possibly predict. For example, supposing one of your star football players is injured and whether he will play is in doubt right up to the last moment before the next game, that is a 'key uncertainty'. If he plays you will probably win and if he is absent you will not. Finally, we flex and interplay the 'key uncertainties' and write the scenarios. The scenarios are no more than simple and consistent stories about the future illustrating the options available.

Thus scenario planning is a straightforward three-part technique, but it is so much more effective than single-line forecasts which offer no understanding of the forces driving the system.

Chart 2 · Structure of the Talk

STRUCTURE OF TALK

The Global Scenarios Produced by an Outside Team of World Experts	The South African Scenarios Produced by Anglo In-House Resources but Modified during Talks

The structure of the book will follow that of the talk. Firstly, we shall deal with the long-term global scenarios. The material comes from an exercise that we undertook during 1985 using a hand-picked team of world experts. It was truly a 'circle of remarkable men', and it is their views which are represented in the global scenarios. In the latter part of the book, we put South Africa in perspective against the global background and assess what options it has. For the South African political and economic scenarios we used the best in-house resources within Anglo. However, because of current events and the sometimes unassailable logic of the responses I have received from the 230 audiences I have addressed, the South African side of the talk has been, and is still being, modified. No one has a monopoly of the truth, and when good ideas are expressed I insert them in the talk. The South African material is therefore more of a composite view now than a single view from the team at Anglo.

PART I
The Global Scenarios

1. The 'Rules of the Game'

The first thing you will notice about this chart is that we divide the world into the 'rich old millions' and the 'poor young billions' or the Triad and the non-Triad. We focus on this distinction rather than the first world and third world, the developing world and developed world. By the Triad we mean broadly North America, Japan and Western Europe. The rest of the world is the non-Triad. Experts are increasingly employing these two terms to denote what they conceive as the true dividing line in the world.

The Triad earns just over two-thirds of the world's income, and has 15 per cent of the world's population living in it – 750 million people out of a total of 5 billion people. Hence, they are rich: the average income inside the Triad is approximately $13 400 a head. In the non-Triad area, you have slightly under 4,3 billion people who earn a little less than a third of the world's income, and their average income

Chart 3 · Future 'Rules of the Game'

FUTURE 'RULES OF THE GAME'

* **Rich Old Millions (Triad)**
  Poor Young Billions (Non-Triad)
* **Africa – the Swamp or the Pit**
* **New Technological Wave – Microelectronics and Biotechnology**
* **Favourable Values Forming**
* **Surplus of Natural Resources and Engineered Commodities**
* **Winners and Losers – Nations and Companies**
* **World Class Companies**

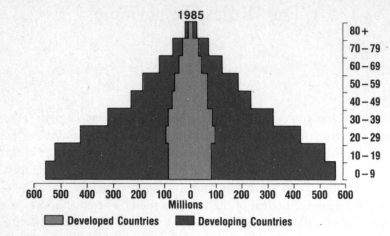

Chart 4 · World Population – 1985

is about $1 100 a head. Hence they are relatively poor. There is a 12:1 income differential between the two areas.

We believe the Triad will continue to be the major market of the world in the 1990s and into the next century, because it has the key to the new technologies where the highest profit potential lies. Nevertheless, some countries such as the newly industrialised Asian ones may successfully emerge to qualify for Triad status at the turn of the century. Brazil is also in with a chance, provided it can overcome its

Chart 5 · World Population – 2005

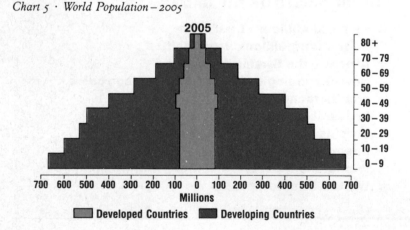

current economic difficulties. Parts of China and India may take off economically by 2005, but it will be well into the next century before their economies match those of the US or Japan.

Now, because Triadians are exposed to ever greater freedom of choice and women are more career-minded, families are becoming smaller. To have a static population in a developed country, you need 210 babies per 100 child-bearing women. In West Germany the rate has fallen to 130 babies; hence the West German population is set to decline by 4 million from 61 million to 57 million people by the year 2005. Most of Western Europe is experiencing a 'baby bust' or 'demographic winter', such that the Western European population as a whole is expected to be virtually static over the next twenty years. The Japanese population is rising very slowly. In the United States growth is more dynamic as the fertility rate is still above the replacement rate and the US is gaining about one million immigrants per year. Western Europe will remain ambivalent to immigrants and Japan will probably keep its doors virtually closed. We see neither the great nineteenth-century migratory waves around the world nor the mass movements to Europe in the 1950s and 1960s repeating themselves in the next twenty years. The only significant migration as regards the Triad will be from and through Mexico into the US.

Thus the population of the Triad as a whole will only expand from 750 million to, we feel, 800 million in 2005, an increase of under 7 per cent, with most of it arising in the United States. The 50 million addition is a very small proportion of the world's overall increase: of the 145 babies being born in the world every minute, six are in the Triad.

As population growth slows in the Triad, so the average age of its population rises. In Switzerland and Japan, for example, around one-fifth of the population will be over 65 in the year 2005. We are in for a 'geriatric boom' in the Triad, and it is going to have important social consequences. At the younger end, the schools are already beginning to empty and youth unemployment will start to fall. There will be less juvenile delinquency because there will be fewer juveniles. In the middle range (especially in Japan), robots will be increasingly evident in production lines, as the active work force declines. At the older

The Ageing of the Japanese Population

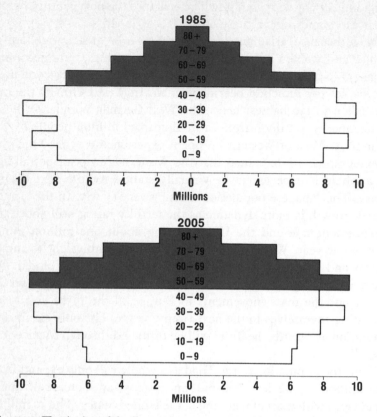

Chart 6 · The Ageing of the Japanese

end, we feel the Triad is going to become more conservative on account of a more elderly profile of voters. Nursing homes will start to multiply: the average life expectancy of a West European woman was 68 in 1955; it is now 78 and it will be over 81 by the year 2000. Already there is a growing controversy about the future adequacy of state health care and pensions. Ultimately, a higher propensity to save may appear among those of working age as the state is forced to diminish its role in the provision of benefits for the elderly.

But the whole point of scenarios is to survey a future which is not fixed. It is possible, as people become more aware of a 'demographic

World Rural Population and Urban Population

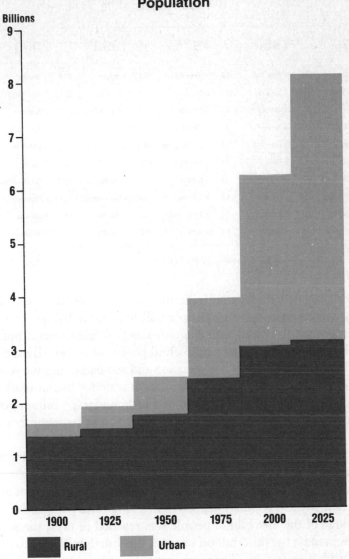

Chart 7 · World Rural and Urban Population

The Ten Largest Cities in the World
1900 – 2000

1900		1950		1975		1990		2000	
1 London	6,5	1 New York	12,3	1 New York	19,8	1 Tokyo	23,4	1 Mexico	31,0
2 New York	4,2	2 London	10,4	2 Tokyo	17,7	2 Mexico	22,9	2 São Paulo	25,8
3 Paris	3,3	3 Rhine-Ruhr	6,9	3 Mexico	11,9	3 New York	21,8	3 Tokyo	24,2
4 Berlin	2,4	4 Tokyo	6,7	4 Shanghai	11,6	4 São Paulo	19,9	4 New York	22,8
5 Chicago	1,8	5 Shanghai	5,8	5 Los Angeles	10,8	5 Shanghai	17,7	5 Shanghai	22,7
6 Vienna	1,7	6 Paris	5,5	6 São Paulo	10,7	6 Peking	15,3	6 Peking	19,9
7 Tokyo	1,5	7 Buenos Aires	5,3	7 London	10,4	7 Rio de Janeiro	14,7	7 Rio de Janeiro	19,0
8 St Petersb'g	1,4	8 Chicago	4,9	8 Buenos Aires	9,3	8 Los Angeles	13,3	8 Bombay	17,1
9 Philadelphia	1,4	9 Moscow	4,8	9 Rhine-Ruhr	9,3	9 Bombay	12,0	9 Calcutta	16,7
10 Manchester	1,2	10 Calcutta	4,4	10 Paris	9,2	10 Calcutta	11,9	10 Djakarta	16,6

Chart 8 · The Ten Largest Cities, 1900–2000

winter' scenario, that a counteracting change in social trends in the 1990s will emerge such that people will have more babies.

We contrast the Triad with the non-Triad. While China is holding its birth rate down with its single-child policy, other non-Triad countries have fertility rates of between 600 and 800 babies per 100 women and in some countries half the population is under fifteen years old. The current non-Triad population of a little under 4,3 billion people will rise to 5,7 billion people in 2005. That is a 34 per cent increase, most of which will be absorbed in urban areas.

By 2000 only two Triad cities, Tokyo and New York, will appear in the ranks of the top ten cities in the world.

In describing future demographics, one would be remiss not to put the whole world's population growth in a long-term perspective. The milestone of the first billion people was reached in 1850, the second billion in 1925, the third billion in 1962, the fourth billion in 1975 and the fifth billion in 1986. The sixth, seventh and eighth billion marks are projected to be passed in 1999, 2009 and 2019 respectively. It is thought that over one-sixth of all the people who have lived since the birth of Christ are alive today. The Triad will fall from 15 per cent to

24

12 per cent of the world's population by the year 2005. Thus, it is going to have to devise jointly with the non-Triad an economic system which benefits the world as a whole. The potential market for consumer goods must eventually shift to where the majority of young consumers live, i.e. the non-Triad. In order to nurture this market, the new economic system will have to incorporate faster technology transfer and freer trade between the Triad and non-Triad.

Africa has the fastest-growing population in the world. Not only is the fertility rate high, but better medicine is reducing infant mortality and increasing life expectancy. The sub-Saharan African population in 1985 was 415 million people, and – barring disasters – it is expected to rise to 840 million people in 2005. That is more than double in twenty years. In some countries, the doubling time is down to seventeen years. By 2005, a little more than one-fifth of the world's under-twenties will be Africans. In 2025 Nigeria is projected to be the fourth most populous nation on earth. Africa's growth in urban population is expected to be nearly twice that of the rest of the world, with 42 per cent of Africa's population being urbanised in 2000. We therefore concentrated on one aspect in Africa – food production.

If one takes the average growth in agricultural production over the last twenty years in the six most populous African countries, and triples it over the next twenty years on account of new technologies, one will still have many people languishing in a 'swamp' of malnutrition. Food production, even accelerated, cannot keep up with the numbers in sub-Saharan Africa. Already it is down 15 per cent per capita on what it was in 1970, whereas China and India have moved to self-sufficiency in food. Asia has 329 million acres of irrigated land against 20 million acres in Africa (one-third of which is in Egypt). If one takes the past average growth in food production and merely extends it forward into the next century, many people will fall into the 'pit' of starvation. The 'swamp' and the 'pit' are not forecasts but scenarios and they certainly do not apply to all sub-Saharan countries. There are successes. Moreover, those in danger can pre-empt the full effect of the scenarios by fundamental changes to their agricultural systems.

The Triad may also ameliorate the situation in the short-term with food aid. Western Europe and the United States have enormous food surpluses in store because of the artificially high prices paid to farmers for their products. In 1986 American farmers, for example, were paid subsidies of about $26 billion, which is nearly double the sum required to keep the entire sub-Saharan population at subsistence level. Western Europe has 1,5 million tons of butter in store and it is feeding the oldest butter to cows in order to recycle it. If all of Western Europe's grain surplus was poured on Lower Manhattan in New York, it would submerge all but the four tallest skyscrapers. The United States had a corn crop in 1985 of nearly 9 billion bushels of which 5 billion bushels were stored. Food hand-outs do not, however, solve the problem in the longer run. The United Nations Environmental Programme quotes that 25 per cent of the 1,7 billion acres of pasture land in Africa has been lost since 1968 and 80 per cent of Africa's range lands has suffered a significant loss in production potential. The focus for development aid in the future must therefore be self-help and conservation projects.

One of the disasters that can overturn any demographic projection is Aids (another is war). All figures on Aids must be treated with great caution because it is such a new disease. However, it is now said that 7 per cent of all Central Africans are sero-positive which means they have been infected with the Aids virus and have the antibodies in their blood, but they have not contracted the disease. That works out at about 5 million sero-positives in Central Africa, of whom between 30 per cent and 70 per cent may contract Aids. Some experts are saying that because the disease has not been around long enough yet, it could be as high as 100 per cent of sero-positives that eventually contract the disease. In some Central African capitals, it is now thought that as many as one in five people is sero-positive. Aids in Africa is called the 'slim' disease and it hits hardest at the twenties and thirties age-groups, who are the breadwinners. The deadly consequence of the Aids virus is that once a person has been infected by it, his or her immune system fails. Other diseases, like TB, can then suddenly come into play. So Aids can open the way to other epidemics.

The figures for Western Europe and the United States are not much less dramatic; there are now three-quarters of a million sero-positives in Western Europe, and 1,5 million in the United States. In the early 1990s there may be between 50 and 100 million sero-positives worldwide. By that time, 54 000 Americans will be dying of Aids each year, more than the annual road casualty toll of 50 000 people, and because of the slow, wasting nature of the disease, the total cost of treating Aids patients will be extremely high (the current cost per patient in America is put at between $50 000 and $150 000).

So, Aids is a vital wild card to consider in the demographic picture. Experts are working on a vaccine, but the problem is that the virus mutates. Hence new strains arise, and this year's vaccine may not be effective against next year's virus. More importantly, the virus hits the immune system, which is the very thing that a vaccine is trying to strengthen to protect a person from catching the disease. Another difficulty is the very high liability risks that companies might face in testing potential products on human beings. Genentech in California, for example, has stated categorically that it will not go ahead with clinical trials unless the state gives immunity from prosecution. Virologists currently surmise that we are at least five years away from a vaccine for Aids and a cure looks to be even further off (although a number of drugs such as AZT appear to slow down the progress of the disease). In the interim, the only thing to do is to educate people. There are some fine programmes underway in Africa, and overseas the dangers have been widely publicised in both Europe and America.

THE NEW TECHNOLOGICAL WAVE

We move on to new technologies. The world is currently going through a burst of innovations, which it does every 40 or 50 years. The last period was in the late 1930s and the early 1940s. It produced such innovations as radar, television, the electron microscope, nylon, the jet aircraft and penicillin. It was this earlier technological ferment that drove the world economy in the 1950s and 1960s. By the 1970s, these technologies had become fully exploited: for the first time in the long post-World War II upswing, the economics of new for old were reversed as technological progress weakened. The escalation in prices of capital goods moved above the general rate of inflation, and the cheapest way of acquiring capacity was to buy existing plant; not to put up new plant. The world economy temporarily stalled. But a new technological wave is here which will drive the system in the 1990s

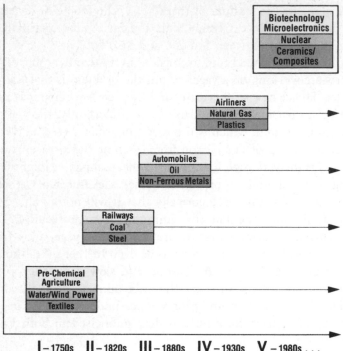

Chart 9 · Long Waves in Technology

and into the next century. We particularly looked at four fields: microelectronics, biotechnology, photonics and ceramics.

Microelectronics had its origin in two innovations which both occurred in the late 1940s: the computer and the transistor. From these products the information age was born. In 1961 the first integrated circuit was produced, and in 1971 the first microprocessor.

We now have so many spin-offs from microelectronics; it has been a blockbuster invention, changing the structure of the world in the same way that the printing press did in the fifteenth century; the steam engine and railways did in the mid-nineteenth century; the car did in the late-nineteenth century; the jet and television set have done in this century; and the fifth-generation computers will do in the next

28

The All Pervading New Tech Wave:
Microprocessors

In Control	Mechanical Systems Process Systems
In Design and Manufacture	CAD/CAM/FMS/CIM* Robotics
In Purchasing and Warehousing	Inventory Control Mechanical Handling Automatic Guided Vehicles
In Retailing	Automatic Checkout/Bar-Coding On-line Price Control Home Shopping Bespoke Products
In Professional Services	Expert Systems Automatic Procedures
In Diagnostics	Expert Systems/A.I.
In Information Transmission/Processing	Distributed Networks Remote Conferencing Office Systems
In Education	Interactive TV/VDU-Based Systems
In Home Entertainment	Interactive Electronic Systems
In Hard/Software Development	'Self-Reinforcement'

*Computer Aided Design/Computer Aided Manufacture/Flexible Manufacturing
Systems/Computer Integrated Manufacturing

Chart 10 · The New Tech Wave – Microprocessors

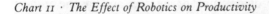

Chart 11 · The Effect of Robotics on Productivity

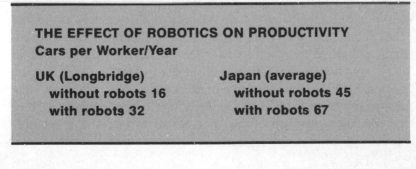

THE EFFECT OF ROBOTICS ON PRODUCTIVITY
Cars per Worker/Year

UK (Longbridge)
   without robots 16
   with robots 32

Japan (average)
   without robots 45
   with robots 67

century. Through microelectronics, the world is designing labour out of the big manufacturing systems and forcing a movement towards service occupations. In the 1950s, 30 per cent of the assembly cost of a car was labour: that figure has fallen to between 7 and 8 per cent as a result of robotics and automated production lines.

In the late 1920s, half of Americans were employed as farmers and blue-collar manufacturers. The figures today are startling. Around 3 per cent of Americans are farmers and 15 per cent are blue-collar manufacturers. About 95 per cent of the new jobs created in the United States in the last ten years have been in the service sector of the economy. The latter now employs 73 per cent of the US workforce. In contrast, the proportion of GNP in the US attributable to the primary and industrial sectors has not shown such a marked decline; in 1950 the aggregate of the two was 46 per cent and in 1984, 34 per cent. This indicates that the productivity gains in these sectors are relatively higher than in services.

Microelectronics is also dispersing people into smaller business units (and in the US away from cities to small towns). Whereas about 50 per cent of Triad workers in the 1950s were employed in big business, the figure has now fallen to about a third. In regard to Japan, we now talk of the 'dual-logic economy', where the 'first logic' economy is constituted by big businesses that offer job security for those lucky enough to be employed by them. A third of these businesses are genuine world champions which earn most of the country's foreign exchange, and they are mainly responsible for Japan's phenomenal success. They have to be huge to compete in the world market. Then there is the 'second logic' economy which is the small-business and informal sector that provides most of the jobs, and has the highest bankruptcy rate in the Triad. Parts of the 'second logic' economy are kept purposely inefficient to keep unemployment down (at the moment about 3 per cent). The retail sector in Japan, for example, has about a hundred thousand more shops than in the United States for half the population. In distribution, generally, there are 5,2 stages, on average, between fabrication of a product and its final sale: in Western Europe the figure is 1,8. The average size of a Japanese farm is three acres. About 9 per cent of the Japanese are farmers, and they only produce 70 per cent of Japanese food requirements. Contrast this with the 3 per cent of Americans who are farmers and produce huge surpluses. The price of rice in Japan is eight to ten times the world market price.

Nevertheless, some small Japanese businesses and even one-man shows are extremely hi-tech. Moreover, big business in Japan positively supports the small-business sector by subcontracting the simpler activities to it. There is a symbiotic relationship between the 'first logic' and 'second logic' economies: they are interwoven.

Here is a marvellous example. In the early 1970s Sony instructed a group of small and medium-sized businesses to miniaturise the components of a machine the size of a large filing cabinet, similar to one used by US TV stations. Each business sent back its miniaturised part to Sony, and Sony assembled the first Betamax video cassette recorder. It appeared on the market in 1975. To this day, the component manufacture of VCRs is done in small and medium-sized business in Japan, whilst big business assembles the whole machine. (At the same time as the parts were miniaturised, Sony reduced the total number required. The result was a more reliable and easy-to-service machine.)

Microelectronics and the 'dual-logic' economy have two crucial messages for South Africa. Firstly, whereas we thought a few years ago that many basic industries would fall into the lap of non-Triad countries because of their relatively cheap labour, we no longer believe that this is necessarily so. The Triad has designed its exorbitant labour costs out of the big systems. Why should Japan locate a car factory in a cheap labour non-Triad country and then pay the freight and insurance for the car to be shipped back to Japan? It makes sense to be close to the customers. The second message is that big business must not only give financial assistance to small-business development, it must positively subcontract the simpler activities as well.

Microelectronics has given birth to two other enormous sectors in today's world economy: the global trading and money markets. Information on commodity prices and exchange rates can in a virtual instant be relayed all round the world. The annual rate of global foreign exchange transactions is estimated at \$85 trillion, a figure nearly six times higher than world GDP and 28 times higher than world visible and invisible trade. These enormous monetary flows, literally at the

The All Pervading New Tech Wave: Biotechnology*

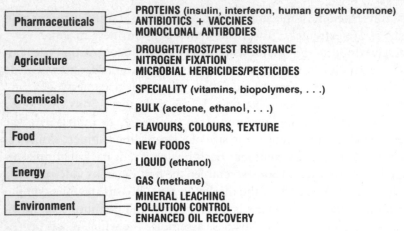

Pharmaceuticals	**PROTEINS** (insulin, interferon, human growth hormone) **ANTIBIOTICS + VACCINES** **MONOCLONAL ANTIBODIES**
Agriculture	**DROUGHT/FROST/PEST RESISTANCE** **NITROGEN FIXATION** **MICROBIAL HERBICIDES/PESTICIDES**
Chemicals	**SPECIALITY** (vitamins, biopolymers, . . .) **BULK** (acetone, ethanol, . . .)
Food	**FLAVOURS, COLOURS, TEXTURE** **NEW FOODS**
Energy	**LIQUID** (ethanol) **GAS** (methane)
Environment	**MINERAL LEACHING** **POLLUTION CONTROL** **ENHANCED OIL RECOVERY**

*PRODUCTS BASED PRINCIPALLY UPON GENE TRANSFER

Chart 12 · The New Tech Wave – Biotechnology

press of a button, now have an inordinate influence on the functioning of the world economy.

Biotechnology today is where microelectronics was ten years ago. The field is not yet living up to its financial promise, but there are undoubtedly long-term pay-offs. Biotechnology is just beginning to take off, particularly in regard to genetic engineering. The scientists take a DNA chain, sever it by using enzymes, insert a new gene, splice it together again and have a living factory capable of producing rare pharmaceutical drugs such as interferon, which is being used in the fight against cancer, and insulin. They recently took DNA from a tobacco plant and inserted a glow-worm gene; now there is a tobacco plant that glows in the dark! In California they think they have isolated the most important constituents of a vintage wine, and they are now genetically engineering vines that may produce vintage wine.

Biotechnology is going to explode in the 1990s, not only in the field of new drugs and frost- and drought-resistant crops; you will have new chemicals, new food flavours, maybe new animals and new enzymes. It is in this last field that there is great potential: they may be able to produce an enzyme that efficiently converts starch into ethanol. Then there will be a renewable source of fuel as opposed to the non-renewable sources of coal and oil. So, biotechnology could have a great impact on the world in the next century.

The third technological field is photonics. Here, information is carried by photons (packets of light) as opposed to electrons, and optical fibre is used as opposed to copper wire. I was recently invited to an optical fibre plant at Brits in the Transvaal. The manager showed me a piece of optical fibre, which looked like a very thin piece of fishing-line. He said that about 2 000 messages could be carried simultaneously on the one fibre. When I asked him how thick the copper wire equivalent for carrying the same number of messages would be, he replied that it would be 5 cm across. So optical fibre is going to replace

Chart 13 · The Impact of the Latest Wave on Existing Industry

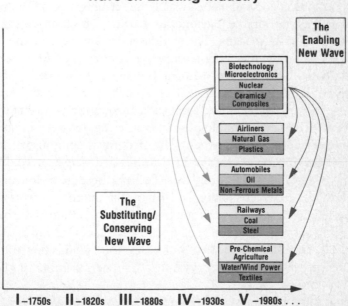

The Impact of the Latest Wave on Existing Industry

most copper telephone wires, and transatlantic and transpacific optical fibre cables are already planned. Equally, optically-driven transistors are being developed which will allow computers to function faster.

The fourth field is ceramics, where companies are coming up with materials which are incredibly resistant to wear and can be used at higher temperature than conventional metals; also with composite materials that are lighter and tougher than aluminium and steel and will therefore replace them. There is even talk of a ceramic car engine one day and super-conducting ceramic cables.

These four technologies will play a dual role, on the one hand enabling some industries to survive through making them more efficient (steel mini-mills in America), while on the other hand causing the demise of others through substitution (possibly compact discs and digital audio tape will replace LPs and conventional tape). They could generate high world growth in the 1990s but other political and economic conditions will need to be fulfilled as well.

SOCIETAL: FAVOURABLE VALUES FORMING

Next, we look at societal values which are forming around the world and which are favourable to economic growth. This section is highly relevant for South Africans. The world is moving away from the belief that a single idea works, that a universal ideology should be used to direct a nation's destiny. Governments are moving towards a pragmatic blend of ideologies: they are taking a pinch of this-ism and a pinch of that-ism, putting them into a pot and concocting a brew that works for them. The new technologies, by scattering people into smaller businesses and self-employment, are making it compulsory to re-examine existing ideologies and institutions that were evolved during the era of huge industrial complexes. Perhaps these are no longer suitable for modern Triad society. In Britain, the number of workers in unions has fallen from 13,3 million in 1979 to 10,7 million at the beginning of 1986. In the US membership of the AFL-CIO union has fallen from 14 to 13 million in the last four years: the union is now offering benefits such as cheap legal services to attract new members and keep existing ones.

I once asked a Japanese businessman, "Are you Socialist or Capitalist in Japan?" and he bluntly replied, "We don't mind whether you call us Socialist or Capitalist: we're just successful. It's you in the West who like to throw abstract cages around things. We don't bother to classify them. We just get on with it." The point is, the Japanese system works for the Japanese, but it will not necessarily work for anyone else. So you have to devise a system that works for you.

In China, Deng has said, "I don't care if a cat is black or white as long as it catches mice." And now he is introducing free enterprise into China, and he will continue to do so, provided it works (and provided the conservative backlash does not stop it). In the Soviet Union, Gorbachev is allowing individual citizens, for the first time, to go into free enterprise in the small service sector. It is a very small step, but it is a start. From the beginning of 1987, Russian companies are being allowed to go into joint ventures with Western companies to earn foreign exchange for Russia. Sovietologists argue over the significance of these moves, but they agree that if, as rumoured, the Politburo passes a law in the near future allowing manufacturing co-operatives to go into free enterprise for the first time, that would be significant.

Gorbachev's whole policy of *glasnost* – openness – runs counter to the Communist practice of central control. In a sense, George Orwell had it wrong, when he implied in *1984* that information gave greater control to the state. Despite the widening web of government and private data bases, the information age actually releases people by giving them the power of knowledge. Gorbachev realises this. In turning the Soviet Union into a modern economy, which uses information-age technology, he will have to decentralise the whole decision-making process and encourage, for example, the widespread use of personal computers. It is ironic that party officials who still support the old brand of communism in Russia are labelled reactionaries. But then a new blend of ideas is being tried out. Some Eastern European countries have acted as pathfinders, such as Hungary which already has a mixed economy of sorts. Lately, Andrei Sakharov mentioned the necessity of converging the socialist and capitalist systems to ensure the lasting peace of mankind.

In Western Europe governments are now elected more on ability to govern and the personalities involved than on clashing ideologies. Most governments in Western Europe are now centrist alliances. In

Spain, Felipe Gonzales was re-elected Spanish prime minister: he is modernising Spain, using free enterprise, and he calls himself a Socialist. In Britain, Neil Kinnock has dropped the word 'nationalisation' from the Labour Party vocabulary, because there are now six million shareholders, including those in the recently privatised British Telecom, British Gas and British Airways, who want to retain their shares. He knows that if he pushes nationalisation, the new shareholders could well vote Conservative. He has mooted an expression called 'Social Ownership'; it is a very involved scheme of turning the shares into loans, but he might even drop that. Meanwhile, the French government has done a U-turn on nationalisation and is handing back companies to the private sector, e.g. Banque Paribas.

In the United States, on a different tack altogether, it is now accepted that the melting-pot theory of forcing people to become homogenised Americans is as bad as forcing people to be ethnically diverse. People are now free to be what they want to be. In Africa, Julius Nyerere has acknowledged that *Ujamaa* in Tanzania was not the success that he had hoped it would be, and Tanzania is making a small start in privatising farming and export industries. Nigeria is following, Kenya is well down the road, and the Organisation of African Unity has recently issued a statement saying there is a positive role for private enterprise in the informal sector of any national economy.

So there we have it. In 600 BC the Chinese were where the world is today when they formulated the *yin-yang* philosophy which states that life is a mixture of opposites – light and dark, good and bad, justice and mercy, and (more relevant to modern times) leadership and participation, competition and co-operation, strength and negotiation, and a loose-tight organisation. In South Africa we are still fighting over 'this-ism' versus 'that-ism', when the world is moving towards 'a bit of each-ism'. That is what South Africa has to do – develop a system that works for South Africans.

THE SURPLUS OF NATURAL RESOURCES AND ENGINEERED COMMODITIES

We now deal with the surplus of natural resources and engineered commodities which has arisen recently. The Club of Rome predicted in its book *Limits to Growth*, first published in 1972, that there would be a growing shortage of raw materials by 1986. People spent billions of dollars on new base metal mines in the hope of steeply rising base metal prices. Of course, nothing could have been more wrong. There was a huge surplus of raw materials in 1986, and commodity prices were at their lowest level in recorded history in relation to prices of manufactured goods and services. The book that should have been written fifteen years ago ought to have been titled *The Growth of Limits* to indicate that we always underestimate the ingenuity of mankind in finding ways around limits. Nevertheless, it should be noted that certain thresholds of importance to ecologists appear to be being crossed: depletion of the ozone layer through use of chlorofluorocarbons; deforestation through acid rain and timber consumption; soil erosion in the non-Triad because land is being too intensively cultivated; the threatened extinction of some animal species in Africa on account of poaching; the warming-up of the world mainly through greater concentration of carbon dioxide in the atmosphere; the growing water shortage in some areas; and the rising number of bacteria and insects resistant to the latest antibiotics and insecticides respectively.

What is happening in relation to raw materials and energy is that the Triad is busy designing them out of the system. The Triad is using 40 per cent less steel per unit of output than in 1970, 36 per cent less oil per unit of output than in 1970. The 7J7 jet that will replace the 737 will consume 40 per cent less aviation fuel, by using the prop-fan engine. The lean-burn car engine, which will use a microprocessor to time the spark in the combustion chamber, will use 25 per cent less petrol than the conventional car engine. A microwave oven uses 5 per cent of the electricity of a conventional oven to cook an identical meal.

The annual growth of consumption of older metals such as copper, zinc and lead has fallen to 0,5 per cent a year and of newer metals such as aluminium and nickel to 1,75 per cent. But base metal producers must not be completely dismayed. A plausible high-growth scenario does exist in which base metals have another day. Some non-Triad countries will go through a metals-intensive phase such as South Korea did in the mid 1960s and 1970s, and the Triad itself will begin to replace much of its old infrastructure. Nevertheless the decline in intensity of consumption inside the Triad will continue.

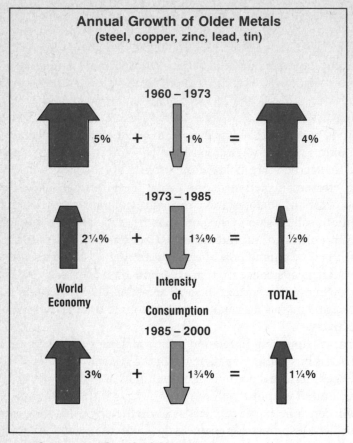

Chart 14 · Consumption Growth of Older Metals

Essentially three megatrends are in play. Firstly, objects like bridges and cars are better designed and have less metal in them. Secondly, the world is moving towards more knowledge-intensive products, which have less raw material content. A microchip, for example, has only 3 per cent raw material content in its cost. And thirdly, the world is moving into services, which have no direct raw material content whatsoever. So we are moving into the 'knowledge-intensive 1990s', where the computer is expanding the boundaries of the mind just as railways, the car and the jet expanded the possibilities of travel.

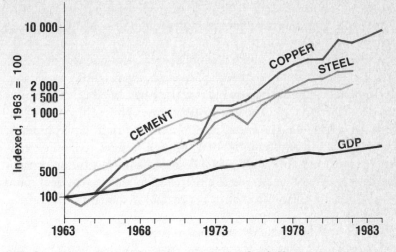

Copper/Cement/Steel/GDP – South Korea

Chart 15 · Copper/Cement/Steel Consumption – South Korea

The future war in the world, in terms of trade, will be fought more on knowledge and less on raw materials. Profit is diminishing on the crude extraction processes upstream and increasing on the sophisticated assembly processes downstream. Australia is a victim of these trends. It has a gross external debt of nearly $65 billion and it is running a current account deficit of around $9 billion a year at the moment. The reason is that the bulk of its exports are primary goods and the terms of trade have moved completely against it. Australian Prime Minister Hawke and Treasurer Keating have both highlighted the foreign exchange crunch facing Australia and the serious consequences for the economy as a whole.

The surplus does not only apply to natural resources; it applies to engineered commodities, i.e. commonly manufactured goods, as well. Around 30 per cent of the world's cars are produced by under 700 000 workers. That is the Japanese car industry. In theory, because of advanced robotics, two million Japanese workers could produce just about all the world's cars. Already Japan produces the majority of the world's VCRs; Taiwan and South Korea between them could probably produce nearly all the world's television sets. It means that in a world of free trade it is no good just producing a product; you have to produce it with a smarter organisation and with higher-tech than your next-door neighbour. It is the only way to make money.

Businesses often focus only on higher-tech. But one wonders how many personal computers there are in large organisations which just prolong inefficient routines by making them easier. Smarter organisation is essential too, like the just-in-time stores philosophy of the Japanese car companies (but you have to have the right environment); and product differentiation is vital through design, reliability, customer service and ultimately price. As regards the last factor, companies have realised that people are prepared to pay a great deal more for quality and reliability than was previously thought.

WINNERS AND LOSERS: 'WINNING NATIONS'

We see stiffer competition leading to a growing divergence between winners and losers at many different levels in the 1990s. We will first ask ourselves what makes a winning and a losing nation, and after examining the formula for success of a nation, we will move on to the phenomenon of 'world-class companies' because each 'winning nation' has its coterie of huge world-class companies that compete on the world stage and earn its foreign exchange. Examples are Nestlé and Brown Boveri of Switzerland; Toyota and Nissan of Japan; and IBM and Boeing of America.

On the brink of the knowledge-intensive 1990s, the foremost characteristic of a 'winning nation' has to be the quality of its education system. I could have covered the chart with education, education, education and education. If you go to the Japanese and ask them, "What is the key to your success?" they will tell you that it is the uniformly high standard of education in Japan in both the rural and urban areas. The Japanese have only 1 per cent functional illiterates versus 13 per cent in America. In 1870, two years after the Meiji Restoration, they set the goal of universal compulsory primary education.

After the Second World War, the target was universal secondary education. An American educational commission recently reported

PORTRAIT OF A 'WINNING NATION'

* **High Education**
* **Work Ethic**
* **Mobilisation of Capital**
* **'Dual-Logic' Economy**
* **Social Harmony**
* **Global Player**

Chart 16 · Portrait of a Winning Nation

that more than 90 per cent of Japanese three- and four-year-olds go to private pre-elementary schools where they are introduced to language, communication and the importance of being a member of a team. Japanese children spend 195 days at school each year compared with 180 days in the United States. However, lessons in Japanese schools were gauged to achieve about one-third more learning than those in American schools. In junior high in Japan, many pupils attend private after-school classes called *juku* for extra exam preparation (and in the holidays too). Teaching is a much sought-after profession in Japan and pay compares well with the private sector. There are five applicants for every teaching position. Ninety per cent of Japanese schoolchildren complete high school.

The adverse side of the Japanese school system is the intensive pressure to work, memorise and conform which leads to a worryingly high rate of bullying and suicides. Interestingly, there is no streaming in either primary or secondary schools but the results are there: in 1970 Japanese children were in top place in both age groups in a series of identical science tests given to ten- and fourteen-year-old children in nineteen countries (the United States was fifteenth overall). The Japanese may also have better young material to educate. In 1982, IQ tests on children between the ages of six and sixteen yielded an average score of 111 for the Japanese compared with 100 for Americans. Ten per cent of Japanese had IQs of 130 or more versus about 2 per cent of Americans (Orientals at Western schools and universities generally top the class).

Education – A Lead Indicator for Technological 'Take-off' The South Korean Example

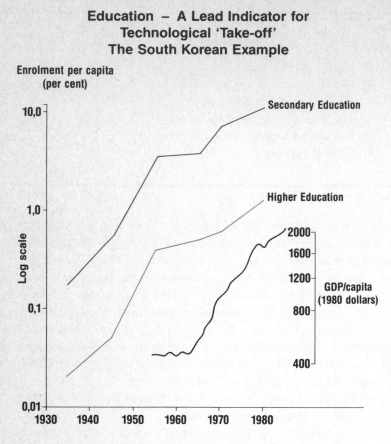

Chart 17 · Education – The South Korean Example

By positively sacrificing consumer expenditure for the sake of educational investment, the South Koreans increased secondary school enrolment from 27 per cent in 1960 to 85 per cent in 1982. Then university enrolment took off, and finally per capita income in the 1970s. South Korea is one of the few players outside the Triad that can compete with the Triad. The fastest-selling imported car of all time in the United States is the Hyundai Excel: it is a South Korean-made car. And the South Koreans are also moving into personal computers, like Daewoo's Leading Edge Model D, which are competing with IBM.

By contrast, the Americans are deeply worried about the decline in quality of their science and mathematics teaching and the shortage of qualified teachers. A 1980 report by the United States Department of Education concluded that the United States now lags behind Russia, Japan and Germany in these disciplines. At the time, there was a sixteen-year consistent decline in SAT scores (tests to qualify for college), even among the top students. Nothing has been published since to suggest a dramatic reversal in this trend. Increasing drop-out rates and absenteeism are also causes for concern.

The position is worse in Britain, Australia, New Zealand and Spain, where only between 50 and 60 per cent of seventeen-year-olds are still at school. For that reason alone, a British educationalist said to me, "Unless Britain jacks up its educational system, Britain is heading for third-world status in the next century." The message for South Africa could not be clearer. Secondary school ratios here are about 89 per cent for whites, 80 per cent for Asians, 44 per cent for coloureds and 35 per cent for blacks. The matric pass rate compared with the total number of eighteen-year-olds is 61 per cent for whites and between 5 per cent and 10 per cent for blacks. That is just not good enough for South Africa to be a 'winning nation' in the knowledge-intensive 1990s, even with a satisfactory political dispensation.

South Africa should probably follow the West German model of keeping all children in the educational system up to the age of eighteen, but splitting them at sixteen years old into two streams: those who will continue with general education and those who will attend technical and vocational courses and apprenticeship schemes. West Germany, as a consequence, has one of the lowest youth unemployment rates in the developed world – 10 per cent versus 22 per cent in Britain. More and more the private sector is also contributing to the cost of education, particularly with adult training programmes for company employees. In the United States, $40 billion is reckoned to be spent on training. Per employee it is over three times more than the British spend but three to four times less than what the Japanese spend.

People in South Africa tend to throw their hands in the air when faced with the size of the education problem. "We cannot double the size of classes," they say, "because that will dramatically lower standards. Therefore we must build far more schools, technikons, universities and teacher training colleges. Where will the money come from? Even then it will take time to train the teachers." The answer is that modern technologies have made it a simpler process to raise general standards of education fast. Screen-based education with videos can supplement normal teacher-to-pupil education. New interactive computer programmes for teaching children are coming onto the market every month. Children like them because they participate in the process of learning. Finally one should create four new TV channels that run virtually throughout the day for pre-primary, primary, secondary and university education. It is through the imaginative use of what is available on the market that South Africa can repeat the South Korean experience. To demonstrate that it is quality rather than quantity of education that counts, the Japanese spend virtually the lowest amount in the Triad on education in terms of percentage of GNP – the figure is 4 per cent (versus 5-6 per cent elsewhere).

It is not adequate to be knowledgeable: you have to work hard too. There are no short cuts. You can make people work hard like Stalin did, or you can create an environment in which they are willing to work. We prefer the latter course. But there are four conditions for people to be willing to work hard.

The first condition is small government; in fact it must be almost invisible. There is a marvellous Chinese proverb: "Govern a great nation like you cook a small fish: don't overdo it." The whole world is moving towards small government. We asked the Japanese MITI (the Ministry of International Trade and Industry), "What is your role vis-à-vis industry?" They said, "We act like a football team coach. We offer tactics, provide the right environment and make sure the pitch is in excellent condition. We don't own the stadium but we keep it in good shape and those guys out there – they win the matches. They are the champions. We don't command them, we help them." Very important. Japan has fewer state employees in relation to its working population than any other member of the Triad – less than half the number in the US, West Germany and Britain. But in Japan it is the cream who enter the civil service.

So the government must act in a support role. In effect the government must be the servant of the people, not the other way around. That is the key. It is in those countries where the government thinks of itself as the champion that the work ethic has declined. People will sit back unless they are given the freedom to do their own thing to fulfil themselves. There is a worldwide trend – backed by the new technologies – towards individual assertiveness, where the individual wants to participate in his own destiny. You can only do that by making government small. In South Africa, people often complain about lack of black entrepreneurial skills. I would direct them to read the first chapter of Leon Louw and Frances Kendall's book *The Solution*. In it, it is shown that a thriving black entrepreneurial spirit existed in South Africa in the nineteenth century, because black people had economic freedom. But from the 1890s they were hemmed in by an increasing network of regulations and entrepreneurship declined. For example, the Glen Grey Act of 1894 restricted black farmers to ten acres each and thenceforth prevented them from competing with white farmers. Pre-1914 Russia exported about 40 per cent of its agricultural output: ever since the state intervened, they have imported food. Sweden is sometimes cited as an exception to the rule that big government can never be a winner, given its recent growth performance. It does indeed have big government from the point of view of spending. But, crucially, the state has the right relationship with the private sector: it allows entrepreneurs the freedom to generate wealth. It does not intervene in the market.

The second condition which contributes to work ethic is a sound family system. In Japan they have this with intensive involvement by mothers in the schooling of their children. In America, between one-third and one-half of all children at some stage in their childhood have experienced a single-parent family, such is the divorce rate (half their marriages in 1987 are expected to end in divorce). A recent survey revealed that 25 per cent of American high school children had used marijuana in the previous 30 days. Crack, an easy way of taking cocaine, is a major problem. We feel that, for that reason, the work ethic is declining in America. If you want to produce children who at the age of eighteen are ready and willing to contribute to society, you have to have a sound family system. In South Africa, the message is that the migratory labour system, which strikes at the heart of the black family system, has to be phased out and better housing for poor families must be provided. In relation to the last point, Singapore turned itself around by embarking on a huge housing programme in the mid-1960s which also helped to cure unemployment.

The third condition that contributes to work ethic is low taxation (this may strike the reader as conflicting with the very last point, but in the end it is a question of balance). The major nations around the world are now competing with one another to reduce rates of income tax. The reason is obvious: if the marginal taxation rate is higher than a certain percentage, people do not want to give that incremental effort, because most of their additional income will go to the government. So America has lowered its marginal tax rate, Britain has slightly dropped its income tax rate, Japan will probably follow and so will others. (However America, to keep its tax rate down, will have to cut government expenditure – the budget deficit demands this.) Countries in future will be competing for capable people to add to their 'knowledge' armoury and successful foreign companies to add to their economy. Low taxation rates are one of the primary sources of attraction.

The fourth condition for work ethic is lack of corruption. In those countries that go beyond a certain level of corruption, the general population says, "What the heck, why should I work, because all the money I earn goes into bribes." So you have to have an open system, that minimises corruption in a country.

But having people who are knowledgeable and work hard is not enough: one has to give them the resources as well. Hence the third factor of a 'winning nation' – mobilisation of capital. Firstly, you have to have a national savings habit. In the Far East people save around 15-20 per cent of their personal income. In Singapore personal savings are higher, because they have a compulsory savings scheme. The figure in South Africa is under 5 per cent. So even with fairly healthy corporate savings this country has to attract foreign capital in order to grow faster. (Right now savings are leaving the country in repayment of foreign debt.) The Far East has by and large used internal savings to grow fast, having learnt the classic macroeconomic equation: savings (local and foreign) equals investment. The Far East, with the possible exception of South Korea, did not need a great deal of foreign capital in order to create its economic miracle.

So South Africa has to create an environment which induces a national savings habit. The first thing is to have positive real interest rates. One cannot ask people to save and in a year's time have them losing out in real terms. But in order to do that, one has to lower the inflation rate, so that when positive real interest rates are created, they are not so high that they turn borrowers off. It is a whole chain of logic that has to be set in motion.

Having obtained the savings, one must have a system that effectively delivers them to where they are most needed. The market economy is the most effective system. But in the small-business and informal sector the commercial risks are often too high for the free enterprise system to deliver. There has to be some other form of delivery system because it is vital for the small-business and informal sector of the economy to get its share of the savings too. One is not talking about hand-outs. One wants an environment in which anyone who wants to become a player and has spotted his niche in the market can gain access to the requisite financial resources.

This brings us to the 'dual-logic' economy. As I explained earlier, we have already moved into an era when the big systems can no longer accommodate all the new work-seekers and unemployment is a major problem. In the Triad the figure stands at 30 million. By 1990 nearly a whole generation (those aged 20-35) will have accepted that it is no longer easy to obtain a job. The comfortable employment conditions of the 1960s are already a distant memory. Just lately in America, General Motors announced that they were laying off 29 000 workers, ATT 27 400 workers and IBM 10 000 workers. The United States steel industry in recent years has shed 300 000 jobs and the car industry about 200 000.

The new technologies have designed blue-collar workers out of the system: they are about to design white-collar workers out of the system with office automation. In France it is estimated that up to 30 per cent of banking and insurance workers could be made redundant by personal computers. And people everywhere will be looking to the small service sector and informal sector for their occupations. The only way to solve the problem is to promote the 'dual-logic' economy. One cannot make job creation per se the objective because, as Adam

Smith said, "Consumption is the sole end and purpose of production." Each job has to satisfy a need. Hence you have to create a system which encourages big and small business into a symbiotic relationship and allows the wealth created in the 'first logic' economy to cascade naturally down through the 'second logic' economy. Italy is becoming one of the more successful countries in Western Europe. Between 20 and 30 per cent of its GDP is earned in the unofficial 'Black Economy' – the informal sector.

On to 'social harmony'. You cannot have one half of a nation at odds with the other half. In Britain they talk of an emerging underclass and of the two Britains: the 'Britain of the North' and the 'Britain of the South'. This division has become clearer over time because of the manufacturing recession in the North, and it could hamper future growth. South Korea and Taiwan are at the moment near to achieving 'winning nation' status. However, they are running ragged at the edges on social harmony. They have to find ways of democratising their institutions, if they are going to become truly 'winning nations'.

If you look around the rest of the world, some of the greatest pain surrounds the issue of minorities. In Sri Lanka it is the Tamils; in Spain the Basques; in America several minorities; in Northern Ireland the Catholics. Alvin Toffler says that the greatest potential for conflict lies with the minorities. For South Africa this 'rule of the game' signals that you must have a constitution acceptable to people as a whole. You certainly cannot have 25 million angry blacks, but neither can you afford to have 3 million angry coloureds and Asians or 5 million angry whites. You have to find something which satisfies South Africans as a whole. We think that is possible, but more will be said when we come to South Africa's future.

Finally, it is those nations that look outwards that win. We looked at nations that look inwards, and they die. We asked the South Koreans, "What has made you so successful, what has changed you from being called 'The Hermit Kingdom'?" They said, "When we looked outwards, and had as our objective climbing the ranks in the world trading system." The South Koreans are now very successful, and they will probably move into the top ten traders of the world in the 1990s. Brazil's manufactured exports increased 25-fold in the period 1970 to 1981, an amazing figure which shows what can be done if you put your mind to it. You have to have a challenge. When the challenge for NASA was landing a man on the moon, it was the finest organisation in the world. Once it had fulfilled the challenge, NASA started coming undone.

We had an American associated with our team, who gave us an intriguing insight into the US. It is called the Big Gorilla Theory. He asked us, "Where does the Big Gorilla sleep?" The team, after consideration, responded, "In the grass." He said, "No." "In the cave?" "No." "In the tree?" "No." So we said we gave up, and he said, "The Big Gorilla sleeps where he wants to sleep." Now the point of that statement is that America has behaved like a big gorilla for years and years, and it has just woken up to the fact that there are two other big gorillas out there in the form of the Japanese and the West Germans. The Americans can no longer put down their bed anywhere they want to put it. They too have realised that they are a global player, subject like everybody else to the discipline of the world economic system. The January 1985 report of President Reagan's Commission on Industrial Competitiveness noted: "Almost one-fifth of our industrial production is exported and fully 70 per cent of the goods we produce compete with merchandise from abroad. Quite simply, no longer is there a truly domestic economy. We are inextricably linked to our trading partners in countless important ways." You have to play by the global 'rules of the game' even if you are a superpower. And so for South Africa to bow out of the global race is the craziest notion of all.

This whole list of factors making up a 'winning nation' may strike the reader as tilting too much towards economic success, and not dealing enough with the conditions necessary for spiritual success. My defence would be that a nation's first duty is to fulfil the lowest needs on the Maslow hierarchy for its population such as security, food and shelter. This it can only do by raising average per capita income. Thereafter other higher-order needs on the Maslow hierarchy can be addressed, though in turning a nation into a winner people will probably satisfy many of their higher-order needs anyway.

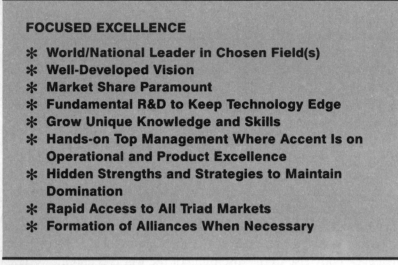

FOCUSED EXCELLENCE

- ✻ **World/National Leader in Chosen Field(s)**
- ✻ **Well-Developed Vision**
- ✻ **Market Share Paramount**
- ✻ **Fundamental R&D to Keep Technology Edge**
- ✻ **Grow Unique Knowledge and Skills**
- ✻ **Hands-on Top Management Where Accent Is on Operational and Product Excellence**
- ✻ **Hidden Strengths and Strategies to Maintain Domination**
- ✻ **Rapid Access to All Triad Markets**
- ✻ **Formation of Alliances When Necessary**

Chart 18 · Focused Excellence

WORLD-CLASS COMPANIES – 'FOCUSED EXCELLENCE'

We then looked at what makes a world-class company. The first thing we noticed is that you can no longer be an all-rounder if you want to be up there at the top: today's world is too competitive. The winners are driven by the principle of 'focused excellence' (this applies to nations as well as companies). They want to be world or national number one in a chosen field, or in a small variety of fields. In the latter case, the South Korean *Chaebols* like Hyundai and Daewoo and the Japanese *Sogo Shosha* like Sumitomo and Mitsubishi are arrays of 'focused excellence' operations. They are not true conglomerates in the Western sense of acquiring a piece of this company and a piece of that company, and growing by acquisition. Far from it: they have grown by carefully nurturing each of their operations.

In the United States, IBM and Boeing are world-class companies. The former wants to be number one in the world in computers but not in aircraft; the latter vice versa. World-class companies have a very well-developed vision of where they want to be in the 1990s. The best example of vision I know of is that of Soichiro Honda, who stood on an orange box in 1948 and lectured his 25 employees in a small garage in Tokyo. He said, "Gentlemen, we are going global", and now he is the largest motorcycle manufacturer in the world; he has fulfilled his vision. Toyota's vision is to increase its share of the world car market from 8 per cent to 10 per cent. There is nothing vague about the vision, it is almost a hard objective. In Japanese companies the primary role of the Chief Executive is to formulate the vision for the company and gain as wide a consensus as possible for that vision by strong leadership but allowing for participation – a good example of *yin-yang*. The vision is then communicated and re-communicated throughout the company to ensure all staff are constantly aware of it. Progress on achieving the vision is briefed too. It makes for a clear sense of direction in a shifting environment and for a consistent strategic planning process.

To world-class companies market share is paramount. The income statement is important, but it is not the key indicator of success; that is market share. For that reason, Japanese export companies have put up their prices in the United States considerably less than the appreciation of the yen would warrant. But they have retained their market share, even at the cost of large knocks to their profit margin. For example, between the first half of 1985 and the first half of 1986, the yen appreciated 40 per cent against the dollar. During the same period, the price of Japanese imported cars rose by 20 per cent, computers by 18 per cent and VCRs fell by 5 per cent. Nissan recently made its first ever half-yearly operating loss. At one talk to a leading industrial company in South Africa the MD said, "You are quite right about market share. In our company we have the credo that as long as we have the customers there must be a way of making money out of them." It is customers that count: they are the top of the pyramid.

Proprietary technology is vital. One cannot live off licensed technology as a world-class company. Many South African companies generate the bulk of their revenue from licensed technologies, but licences can be restricted (particularly in terms of target markets), or terminated. In the end, you must develop a lot of your own proprietary technology. You have to 'grow' your people and skills over a long period of time. You have to have a 'hands-on' top management who understand the soul of the business and whose accent is on operational and product excellence. The money then looks after itself. That is why there are so few state-owned world-class companies; it is because bureaucrats do not make good entrepreneurs. The world is realising this – hence the reversal to private ownership of state industries in many countries, Triad and non-Triad alike (the largest recently is Japan's Nippon Telegraph and Telephone which had a debut market capitalisation of $164 billion).

In Japan, they have this image of the company as a tree, where the roots represent the technologies that provide nourishment and stability, the trunk the people and skills which are uniquely the company's own, the branches the activities and the fruits the products. The tree has great symbolic significance in the Shinto religion, as it is where the divinities dwell. In industry it takes 25 years to grow a decent tree: that is the Japanese thinking. In terms of hidden strengths and strategies, the Japanese have a term which roughly translated means 'invisible assets'. This is your people, your accumulation of skills and knowledge, your culture, your design, your market and product research and your software; those things that are invisible to your com-

Chart 19 · The Japanese Image of the Company as a Tree

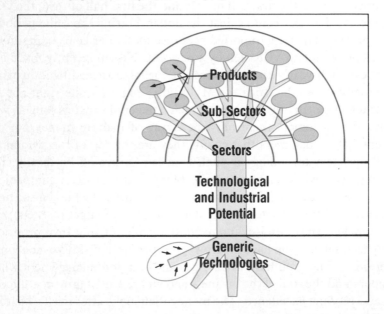

petitors. And Japanese companies are building up this reservoir of 'invisible assets' to unleash on their competitors, because, as I said earlier on, the world trade battle is going to be fought more and more on knowledge and less and less on raw materials. People will count more than buildings and plant, and the Japanese are the first to tumble to that. They now invest more in 'invisible assets' than the visible assets which appear on the balance sheet. The strategy is to keep your 'invisible assets' out of sight of your competitors, while making sure they cannot develop their own.

Here is a glorious example. In 1982, Honda was challenged by Yamaha for leadership of the motorcycle market. Honda had 39 per cent and Yamaha 34 per cent. Yamaha said, "We are building a new factory, capable of producing 2 million motorcycles a year, and we are going to become the number one in Japan in a year and the number one in the world in two years." What did Honda do? It wheeled out, over an eighteen-month period, 81 new varieties of motorcycle covering every single niche of the market, dropped its prices dramatically, and spent heavily on promotion. Yamaha took a beating and its market share dropped by 9 percentage points. The president of Yamaha had to apologise publicly to the president of Honda; he had to resign, and the factory was never completed. That was Honda unleashing its 'invisible assets' on Yamaha, and that is what it takes to be a world-class company. Those 81 new designs did not appear out of thin air – they were kept in the bottom drawer in case of a threat, which materialised.

World-class companies are now developing inside operations in the three legs of the Triad. The strategy is no longer to export from Japan into Europe and from Europe into the United States; you have an integrated manufacturing process in all three areas. For Japanese companies it is most important, with the hardening yen, to move overseas. Nissan, for example, recently opened a plant in the north-east of England. Apart from potentially cheaper manufacturing costs, the reason is that if the British ever put up trade barriers against Japanese cars, Nissan is there, working from inside the British economy.

Another reason for being an insider in all three areas is that the Triad is moving towards being a universal market. Young people wear Sony Walkmans in Japan, in Western Europe and in the United

COMPANY SURVEY

77 of the World's Top 100 Companies and All but One of Japan's Top 50 Companies Follow Focused Excellence Principles (Including Sogo Shosha)

Chart 20 · Company Survey

States; they wear the same Levi jeans; they buy the same compact disc players and video camcorders. Hence when one produces a new product, it no longer has to be individually stylised for each area of the Triad. One blitzes the entire Triad with virtually the identical product. And the pace of technological catch-up has now become so fast that a company has to make most of its money in three to six months on, say, a new electronics product, because after that its competitors will have produced a competitive look-alike for the market.

And finally, world-class companies form alliances crisscrossing the whole Triad. It is much easier to go into partnership with a company which has a major market share in another area of the Triad and an established marketing network than to carve out that market share and network for yourself. Equally, research and development costs on a new high-tech product are reaching such astronomic proportions that the costs must be shared between several companies working in alliance. For example, ATT from the United States has formed an alliance with Olivetti to market telecommunications equipment in Western Europe and the US; while Daewoo from South Korea has formed an alliance with General Motors to market the new Le Mans car in America. Toyota have allied with General Motors to produce the small Nova car in California (under Toyota management). The best illustration in favour of alliances was the way Matsushita and its half-owned subsidiary JVC cornered the VCR market through sharing its invention with others. Sony did not. The result: 90 per cent of the 100 million VCRs ever sold have been of the Matsushita VHS type.

The proof of the pudding is in the eating. We did a very rough survey, which showed that 77 of the world's top 100 companies and all but one of Japan's top 50 companies follow the 'focused excellence' principle (including the *Sogo Shosha*).

Of the other twenty-three, which are classed as conglomerates in the world rankings, most are diversifying out of ageing trees; they are acquiring other companies because their core business is declining. For example, BATS and Philip Morris are moving out of tobacco. There are only a few genuine conglomerates left in the top 100; for example IRI which is a state-owned Italian conglomerate and ITT – International Telephone and Telegraph – which is an American conglomerate. But ITT has sold 94 of its businesses; it has reduced itself to more of a 'focused excellence' operation. Another glamorous conglomerate of the 1960s, LTV or Ling Temco Voight, has just filed under Chapter 11 for bankruptcy. So the old myth of it being easy to grow big by being a conglomerate has been completely shattered in the 1970s and 1980s. You have to focus your excellence. A recent study by Harvard Business School showed that two-thirds of unrelated businesses bought by 33 big American companies were later resold.

2. The Three Main Actors

This brings us to a description of the three main actors in the world as one moves into the 1990s. We chose Japan, the United States and the Soviet Union. "Where is Western Europe?" you might say. "After all, it is part of the Triad." After careful consideration, and despite the obvious importance of West Germany as an economic actor, we decided that the world's destiny over the remainder of this century will pivot on the relationships between the United States and the Soviet Union, and between the United States and Japan.

Western Europe is losing ground in the technology race because it is not yet combining its manifold resources. For example, there has not been one single trans-European company of note formed since the Common Market was established. Shell and Unilever were founded prior to 1957. The nearest to a wholly Western European company is IBM Europe, which is an American company. An oft-quoted exception to this statement is Airbus Industrie, the European four-nation consortium, which manufactures large passenger aircraft. It is reckoned that Airbus's latest product, the A320, is very competitive, and its next generation of airliners, the A330 and A340, will compete with anything Boeing and McDonnell Douglas will produce. Nevertheless, Airbus has yet to turn a profit after seventeen years in business: indeed it could not have stayed in business but for the $10 billion of aid from European taxpayers.

The majority of the highest-tech electronics goods now sold in Western Europe are sourced from Japan and the United States; the only truly European players in consumer high-tech electronics are Philips and Olivetti. Overall in electronics – that is in telecommunications, industrial automation, computers and office automation, components and consumer electronics – Western Europe is running a substantial trade deficit. For the first time in modern history, Western Europe is not riding out front on the crest of a new wave in technology. On the contrary, it is lagging behind. If they are to avoid eventually falling off the radar screen, the West Europeans will have to

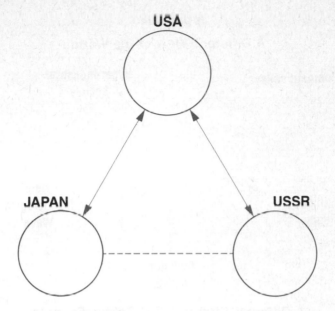

Chart 21 · The Three Main Actors

turn to advantage their differing nationalisms and languages. There are signs that they are doing so. But an important lesson to be learned from the Western European experience is that fragmentation into small-nation states seriously impedes progress in the world game.

JAPAN

The Japanese are ultra-competitive, in a way that many people outside Japan do not understand. This flows from the fact that Japanese children are taught, from the day they enter nursery school, that Japan is a poor nation; it has no raw materials, it must import everything, even food, and it is only by dint of working hard and gathering knowledge that the Japanese have become as successful as they are.

Japan has three hundred million people on its doorstep trying to emulate it. We are talking of those Pacific Rim countries which are climbing the lower rungs of the technology ladder, and the Japanese have to climb the higher rungs that much faster. Moreover, Taiwanese and South Korean workers are prepared to do the same jobs as Japanese workers for one-sixth of the wages. The recent rise in the yen has

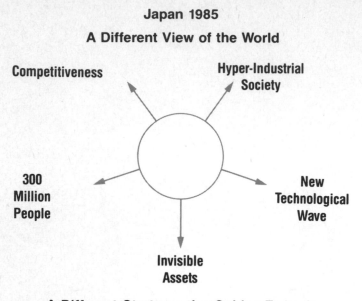

Japan 1985
A Different View of the World

Competitiveness

Hyper-Industrial
Society

300
Million
People

New
Technological
Wave

Invisible
Assets

A Different Strategy: the Golden Formula

Chart 22 · Japan

given such newly-industrialised countries as Taiwan and South Korea an extra advantage in the fiercely competitive game of exporting goods to the world. Their currencies have not appreciated significantly against the dollar; hence they are gaining market share from the Japanese in such fields as shipbuilding, steel and TV sets. For example, Japan's share of the world shipbuilding market fell from 49 per cent in 1985 to about 42 per cent in 1986 while South Korea's rose from 10 per cent to 28 per cent.

The success of the Japanese has rested on their belief in creating a hyper-industrial society while the rest of the Triad becomes post-industrial. About 20 per cent of college students in Japan are in engineering; in the United States the proportion is below 5 per cent. In secondary schools in Japan almost 40 per cent of pupils study engineering. Japan's share of world exports of manufactured goods has recently been 13 per cent; its share of world imports of manufactures is only 3 per cent (it only imports slightly more manufactures than

Switzerland, whose population is 6,6 million compared with 120 million in Japan). The gap between Japan's share of world manufactured exports and imports, which used to be in the range 4 to 5 per cent, roughly similar to that of Germany, is about 10 to 11 per cent. Of course the appreciation of the yen will probably narrow the gap again, though it has not done so in the short term. Japan already produces 50 per cent more industrial goods per capita than the United States. The combination of a hitherto undervalued yen, high savings for investment and falling real wages per unit of output in manufacturing has ensured the competitiveness of Japanese industry.

The Japanese believe in their manufacturing champions, like Toyota, Sony and Nissan; they have provided Japan with an $86 billion current account surplus in 1986, and Japan has the lion's share of international lending. So, nine of the world's ten biggest banks, measured by assets, are now Japanese. Number one is Daichi Kangyo (if one excludes the Post Office Savings Bank in Japan), number two is Fuji, and thereafter follow Sumitomo, Mitsubishi and Sanwa. Only then comes Citicorp (US), and the next four are Japanese again.

In financial services the number one company in Japan is Nomura Securities; its market capitalisation is about $30 billion. It is five times the size of Goldman Sachs or Salomon Brothers, the largest investment houses in the United States. *The Economist* said that Nomura could, with relative ease, take over all the top sixteen merchant banks in the UK. The Japanese are therefore using their industrial triumphs to take the number one positions in the financial sector as well.

The Japanese spend more money on research on the new technological wave for consumers than any other nation. The United States still spends about 50 per cent of its research on defence and space; the Japanese spend virtually 100 per cent of their research on being an economic superpower. In Japan the sense and the reality of the new wave is so strong that a 'zero investment' approach to growth in production capacity has emerged; it pays to look at past investment as if it did not exist. Matsushita about two years ago scrapped a plant that was three and a half years old in order to replace it with a new plant equipped with the latest technology.

One field that we examined was the fifth-generation computer. This is going to be the key to the 1990s because of the incredible uses to which it can be put by such diverse consumers as big business and housewives. The computer will be able to recognise handwritten text and transcribe it onto the screen. It will recognise your voice; you will be able to talk to it and your words will appear on the screen. Indeed in Japan there is now an example of a computer where you talk to it in English and the script appears on the screen in Japanese. You will be able to design an entire aircraft on this computer and rotate it in three dimensions, with a fifth-generation CAD/CAM. You will be able to test-fly it on the computer, because the computer will calculate all the stresses and strains on the wings and fuselage, so it will cut down design time and the use of physical models and wind tunnels. The computer will self-program all simple functions and it is only the highest order inference functions and knowledge of experts that will have to be fed into it. A housewife will be able to switch the machine on and demand (vocally) the prices of today's vegetables in town. Within seconds, the data will be on the screen. In other words it will become a universal household gadget, which the fourth generation never achieved because there has to be some learning to use it.

Now the Japanese have had two projects going hand in hand since 1982: the 'supercomputer' project to develop the fastest computer in the world, and the fifth-generation project to develop the most intelligent computer. They have produced systems of microprocessors working in parallel which have achieved the same speed as the fastest supercomputers in the United States. IBM are very worried about the Japanese threat. The Japanese are so thorough. They have software libraries full of re-usable codes. There is no re-inventing the wheel as there tends to be in the United States. You take the software information to date and you innovate on that information; that is the key to Japanese success.

'Invisible assets' were described earlier. The Japanese are the first nation to realise that it is their reservoir of 'invisible assets' which really counts as they go into the 1990s (which makes the brain drain so critical for South Africa – estimated in 1986 as a net loss of three professional people a day). The Japanese intend to push further in fields such as office automation, biotechnology and telecommunications. They want to broaden their range of brilliant world-class companies; less than 200 companies account for 75 per cent of Japan's exports, the equivalent figure in West Germany being 4 500.

Lastly, on account of the much stronger yen, Japan is going through a major re-think of its strategy. From 1980 to 1984 the external sector provided some 40 per cent of Japan's total GNP growth. In 1985 the proportion was near 50 per cent. In 1986 net export growth was negative and the increase in GNP (2,1 per cent) came entirely from domestic demand. The higher yen has definitely hurt the Japanese economy by slowing growth and raising unemployment. Steel, coal-mining, shipbuilding and the textile industry are all laying off large numbers of workers. Components of the new strategy, we think, will be greater emphasis on stimulating internal demand, raising the quality of life in Japan and increasing Japan's direct investments in other Triad and non-Triad countries.

Surprisingly, the one thing that terrifies Japan is the possibility of a devastating earthquake during the scenario period.

USA

The Americans have been the most successful nation in the world in the twentieth century, but like any institution that has been at the top for a lengthy period they are concerned about losing their position. They have good points and bad points. Let us take the good points first.

Above all, there is an entrepreneurial revolution going on in America, where the hippies of the 1960s – the young people who went to San Francisco and wore flowers in their hair – are now the 'yuppies' of the 1980s, the young upwardly mobile professionals. It is a societal rather than an economic phenomenon, in that the 'baby boom' generation, who in the 1960s were demonstrating against Vietnam, are now finding a more constructive outlet in creating their own businesses. They do it not so much to make money but to express their personality. The movement is very evident on the campuses which were formerly the focus of discontent. And they are completely transforming the small service sector of the American economy; the mom-and-pop food shops, barber shops, shoe repair shops – basic services. Hi-tech companies represent only 12 per cent of new business creation. The Harvard Business School's students used to join the big companies;

```
USA

*  Change in Mood/Societal Revolution
*  Job Creation
*  Influx of Capital
*  Centres of Excellence
*  Migrants
but
*  Low Productivity Growth
*  Low Savings
*  Twin Deficits
*  Non-Participative Management Style
*  Obsession with Short Term
```

Chart 23 · USA

now 85 per cent of graduates want to create their own companies. They may temporarily join a bank or consulting firm to earn the money to repay their tuition fees, but their ambition is to start up in business for themselves. Now large companies are seeking to capitalise on the movement by emphasising 'intra-preneurship', i.e. fostering entrepreneurs inside their own corporate structures. If they succeed in this, the prospects for long-term reinvigoration of the United States economy generally will be greatly improved. The United States' drive for business innovation as self-expression could be as powerful in its economic impact as the group motivation of the Japanese to prove to the world that Japan is best.

Secondly, the United States is still a job-creation machine. It has created over 30 million new jobs since 1970. In Western Europe the net figure is almost zero during the same period; for every service job gained there has been a manufacturing job lost. Hence the West European unemployment rate is running at 11 per cent, whereas in the United States it is running at 6,7 per cent.

The United States still receives a great deal of savings from the rest of the world in loans and investment; it is still regarded as the safest haven. The Japanese are investing heavily in America; they spent $27 billion in 1986 on plant, equipment and real estate and at least $65 billion on dollar bonds. It is estimated that one quarter of a million Americans now work for Japanese firms in the United States and this figure could rise to over one million in ten years.

America still has the best universities in the world: Harvard, Yale, Princeton, UCLA, Berkeley, Chicago, MIT, Houston. One of the acid tests is that the Japanese send their smartest graduates there to finish their education, and then they go back to Japan. The Chinese do the same, but many remain in the United States. A lot of the most talented university staff from Britain and other European countries emigrate to American universities, because of the superb facilities they have and the attractive salaries they pay. It is important to realise why the best universities in the Triad have in effect broadened themselves into 'centres of excellence'. Since knowledge is such a key factor to a nation in the 1990s, these universities now perform a dual function of teaching students on the one hand, and acting as a source of inspiration to the private sector on the other. They provide the seeds for new entrepreneurial activities and co-operate closely with big business on basic research. Japanese companies have recently funded nine chairs at Massachusetts Institute of Technology in areas such as ceramics, management and communication. The role of the university in South Africa needs to be re-conceptualised for the same reasons.

America believes in 'richness in diversity', whereas the Japanese believe in 'strength in homogeneity'. The United States positively attracts successive waves of migrants who bring new blood into the economy; Japan accepts few migrants. The latest wave in the United States is made up of Orientals, particularly South Koreans, who are transforming the Californian economy. Asian Americans account for 11 per cent of the 1987 freshman class at universities while they only make up 2 per cent of the nation's college-age population. Equally, between 500 000 and one million Mexicans will move into the United States legally and illegally this year, though the number appears to be falling because of the new immigration act. The United States is now the fifth-largest Spanish-speaking nation on earth. Los Angeles is second to Mexico City in terms of concentration of Mexicans and a large proportion of Miami is Cuban. Problems are arising in California, where most Spanish-speaking Americans are located, because people are asking for Spanish to be a second official language, and for it to be used as the medium of education at schools. Nevertheless, America has always come up with imaginative solutions, and there is no reason why it should move away from the heterogeneous model which has been the backbone of its success this century. South Africans often ask how this country can be an economic success with such a heterogeneous population. The answer is that the Americans have managed to create a model that works for them (and so have the Swiss who are the richest country in Western Europe). One must not only focus on the Japanese model, which of course works for the Japanese but is not necessarily appropriate elsewhere.

On the negative side, the United States has very low productivity growth; it may be related to declining work ethic. Alone among the Triad, the United States has shown no acceleration in its productivity growth (output per man hour) after the Second World War. Over the past two decades, United States productivity growth has compared poorly with the UK and is some five times below Japanese growth. It is no longer possible to attribute this poor performance to a 'catch-up' process. Indeed, Japan's growth is strongest in those industries which have already overtaken United States productivity levels. The same point is clear from direct comparison of even well-managed American companies with their Japanese competitors. For instance, Komatsu in 1978 produced 20 per cent less per employee than Caterpillar. Their relative positions have since reversed. Similarly, GE had – at least until recently – an increase in productivity only half that of Hitachi and indeed well below that of its better West European rivals. The average annual increase in productivity in the manufacture of electrical machinery was 4,5 per cent in the United States, 7,9 per cent in Holland and 13,2 per cent in Japan from 1975 to 1983. In December 1986 a group of United States industrialists, labour leaders and academics launched the Council on Competitiveness. So the problem of low productivity growth is now clearly perceived.

The US has a very low savings rate. Americans save only 5 per cent of their personal income, whereas the Japanese save 16 per cent of theirs. As one Harvard professor put it to us, "The Japanese operate

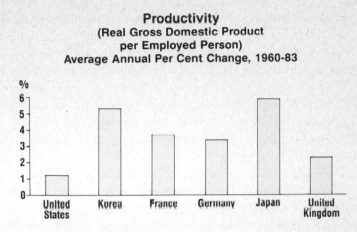

Productivity
(Real Gross Domestic Product
per Employed Person)
Average Annual Per Cent Change, 1960-83

Chart 24 · Productivity Growth, 1960-1983

on producer logic whereas we operate on consumer logic." Part of the explanation is the way in which the US tax system, even the new one, penalises saving in favour of consumption. This bias has been present for decades. At the end of World War II the US, contrary to Western Europe and Japan, emerged with its full productive capacity intact. The policy concern was to ensure sufficient demand to maintain output near capacity. As a result, the tax system in the US was geared to subsidising consumption while in Western Europe, and even more so in Japan, the opposite was the case. And it is because of the consumer-orientated society that the Americans have two enormous deficits: the trade deficit of $170 billion and the budget deficit of $220 billion. They have to face up to the fact that they are spending beyond their means. Either they are going to return to a balanced position slowly and purposefully, or they are going to experience some sharp discontinuities in their economic growth.

The US has talked about participative management for years, but still many assembly-line workers in the States just assemble. In the words of a Japanese observer, "You Americans still believe that managers know more than workers; this used to be true in the last industrial age but now the discretionary power of workers has dramatically increased. They know much more than managers where progress can be achieved." The American company is handicapped in the race to develop 'invisible assets' precisely because American workers are so mobile – they change jobs for marginal improvement in conditions. The feeling is that it does not make sense to invest in assets which will probably walk away. In Japan, workers contribute to management through quality circles; there are now estimated to be 600 000 quality circles covering 6 million employees (*yin-yang* – the CEO in Japan is still very much the boss, but they have participation). That is one reason why the quality of Japanese products has risen so dramatically in relation to those of the rest of the world. Recent consumer polls in the US on the technical reliability of cars almost always have a Japanese car topping them. The average repairs on a Japanese car are estimated at 1,1 per year against 3,5 for an American car.

And finally there is the obsession with the short term: the US believes in the 'quick fix'. Investment fund managers put pressure on company operating management to produce excellent quarterly results. The strategy of most companies in America is therefore driven by quarterly results. It is called 'quarteritis', and it is no match for the Japanese twenty-five year strategy of growing trees. An example makes the point. In July 1984, ITT announced its intention to reduce dividends for a temporary period in order to finance the investment required to re-enter the US market for telecommunications. The company was confident that this strategy was sound and its view was shared by much of the business press. Nevertheless, the response of fund managers, who were already worried by some aspects of ITT's business performance, was immediate and hostile. The ITT share price plummeted, dropping by one third in the first day's trading after the announcement of the company's plans which, soon after, were abandoned. According to an estimate made for the New York Stock Exchange, the average length of institutional holding of stock in American bluechip companies is four months and seventeen days. The management of some companies is buying back stock from the public to regain private status for their companies. Management can then pursue long-term goals unhampered by public opinion.

One has to ask oneself whether a nation like the US is behaving unusually at this point in its evolution. The answer is no – there are two 'laws of nations'. The first 'law' is that no nation in the world has held the number one position for long, and the second 'law' is that no nation that has lost the number one position has ever regained it.

In 1650, the Dutch were the manufacturing champions of the world; by 1750 they had become a nation of traders and financiers, and it was Britain's turn to take off. In the late 1700s the British began their industrial revolution, but in 1870 they peaked at 32 per cent of world output. By this time the British had turned their attention more to administering the Empire than retaining their manufacturing excellence. Next it was the Americans' turn to take off, and by the late 1920s they had risen to 42 per cent of world output. Thereafter the US consistently declined and now represents 29 per cent of the world output (and Britain 4 per cent) versus Japan which is now 15 per cent. History may not repeat itself but the Japanese have become the world's greatest banking nation. By the year 2000, Japan will probably have a trillion dollars' worth of assets overseas, on which it will earn vast invisible income (similar to the British experience at the beginning of this century). It could by then have a declining manufacturing core at home, and it too will start to decline. Who knows who it will be next century? It might well be the Chinese, for the first come-back ever, in 2050. Or perhaps the world will experience a leadership vacuum: there will be no clear leaders, in which case success will rest on a harmonious and co-operative relationship between a whole group of 'winning nations'.

Nations rise and fall; they start out in manufacturing excellence and end up as rentiers. The best brains move from physical to financial engineering. It must be something to do with the challenge receding once you are at the top. The drive is no longer there (it applies to companies too). Where is Egypt now? It used to possess the leading edge of civilisation in Alexandria. Where are the Greeks? They were once at the forefront of mathematics and philosophy. Where are the invincible Romans? They all vanish.

So the idea that a superpower can actually stay at the top forever is certainly not proven by the history of mankind.

Before moving on to Russia, we should compare the American model of doing business with the Japanese model. In America, you have no master plan, you rely on individual brilliance, and individual kudos drives the system. Steven Jobs is an archetypal American hero: he is a college drop-out who invented the personal computer. The US

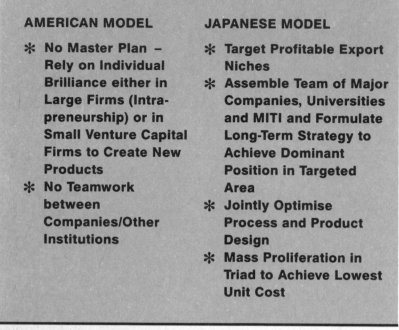

AMERICAN MODEL	JAPANESE MODEL
* No Master Plan – Rely on Individual Brilliance either in Large Firms (Intrapreneurship) or in Small Venture Capital Firms to Create New Products * No Teamwork between Companies/Other Institutions	* Target Profitable Export Niches * Assemble Team of Major Companies, Universities and MITI and Formulate Long-Term Strategy to Achieve Dominant Position in Targeted Area * Jointly Optimise Process and Product Design * Mass Proliferation in Triad to Achieve Lowest Unit Cost

Chart 25 · American Model/Japanese Model

has won 130 Nobel Prizes in science, whereas the Japanese have only won four (Cambridge's Cavendish laboratory in England has produced over 80). In that sense there are individuals in the US at the pinnacle of their specialisations. But Japan does not focus on Nobel prizes. Because of the consistently high level of their education system, the middle 80 per cent of Japanese are well ahead of the middle 80 per cent of the United States; that is what counts in industry.

There is no teamwork between US companies because it is regarded as illegal collusion. In Japan you target an export niche; you assemble a team of major companies, universities and MITI and you jointly formulate the long-term strategy. You jointly optimise the process and product design, and then you severally mass-proliferate the product throughout the Triad to achieve lowest unit cost. This model almost without exception defeats the US model; it is another example of *yin-yang*, each firm co-operating to begin with, then in the last step competing with one another. In the late 1960s it was colour TV sets which were showered on the US as a result of teamwork between major Japanese consumer electronic companies. In the mid-1970s it was microchips, the 'rice of industry', arising from the very large scale integration (VLSI) project put together by MITI. The Japanese moved swiftly from 16K ram chips in the late 1970s to 64K ram chips in 1981, which were still fairly crude, to 256K ram chips in 1983 which in quality – because of automated production processes – were better than the American product. Needless to say, Japan is in the lead in developing megabit chips. In the early 1980s, it was numerically-controlled machine tools, the Japanese quickly capturing 60 per cent of the world market. Now it is the fifth-generation computer.

In the US the accusation has been levelled at the Japanese that they take American basic ideas, thoroughly innovate on them and then manufacture superb products without justly rewarding the original inventors (the British once said the same about the Americans). Moreover, the US is becoming increasingly angry that its companies are suffering from the red-hot competition of Japanese firms exploiting American ideas. The Japanese, on the other hand, argue that they are providing sophisticated products at the cheapest possible cost for countless American consumers, who otherwise would not have been able to buy them. Nobody is forcing people to buy Japanese products.

As you will see, one of our 'key uncertainties' is whether the US and Japan seek an accommodation with one another or precipitate a trade war. One of the essential points of that relationship is how knowledge is going to be transferred in future between America and Japan.

USSR

Gorbachev appears to be beginning to turn Russia around, though sceptics will comment that it is too early to say. In the 1960s, GDP growth per capita was running at 3,5 to 4,3 per cent a year. It gradually fell to an average of just over 1 per cent a year in 1981-1985 (*Pravda* recently published an article implying that growth was actually negative in the latter part of the Brezhnev era). But in 1986, grain, coal and oil production all rose. Part of the reason stems from the govern-

USSR

* Deterioration in GDP Growth per Capita
* Decline in Labour Force in European Russia
* Declining Productivity of Capital
* Acute Shortage of Foreign Exchange
* Growing Handicap of Central Planning
  for Complex Economy

but

* Vast Potential Consumer Demand

Chart 26 · USSR

ment's programme against alcoholism; vodka consumption is said to have halved in the last two years.

There are three major constraints to the Soviet economy, however. The first is manpower. The labour force in European Russia has fallen in absolute terms since 1980, and is projected to continue declining until the mid-1990s. In fact, the European Russians are declining as a proportion of the overall population because their birthrate is well below that of the Soviet population in the East and the Asian Republics of the South. This poses not only the problem of a changing skills mix in the labour force, but also a conundrum about future power, since the European Russians have controlled the Soviet Union since the Revolution.

The second constraint is declining productivity of capital. During the first two post-war decades the capital co-efficient, i.e. the amount of investment required to raise GNP by 1 per cent, fluctuated narrowly around an average value of 1,6. In the first half of the 1970s the efficiency of investment fell by 30 per cent and subsequently dropped dramatically, so that the capital co-efficient now is near 3,5, double its earlier level. The deterioration is the result of several factors. First, there is the problem of agriculture. In the US the agricultural sector accounts for only 6 per cent of total investment; in the Soviet Union agriculture absorbs 27 per cent of it. Second, the shift in the resource

70

base to West Siberia (especially oil, since the more easily accessible oil-fields west of the Urals are beginning to be exhausted) requires heavy investment in infrastructure and increased transport costs in moving men and materials. Moreover, by and large, new resources are of poorer quality. An estimate produced recently in Washington by a firm which tracks economies in the Soviet Union and Eastern Europe puts the cost of developing a Siberian oil well at $45 a barrel – well above the current oil price.

The third constraint is an acute shortage of foreign exchange. That really relates to oil too. The Soviet economy was saved by the two oil shocks of the 1970s. Prior to 1973, energy exports provided 12 per cent to 15 per cent of Russia's hard currency earnings. However, hydrocarbons from 1982 to 1984 accounted for 80 per cent of Russia's exports to the Triad, with oil alone providing 64 per cent of the total ($16 billion out of $25 billion a year total foreign exchange earnings). Because of the increase in energy prices the Soviet Union has been able to im-

Chart 27 · Soviet GDP, 1961-1990

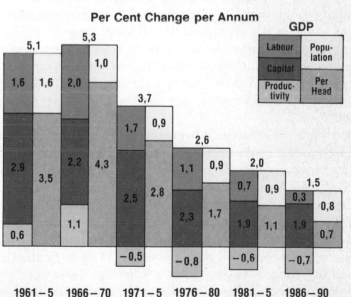

Soviet GDP (1961 – 1990)

Per Cent Change per Annum

port food and Western equipment and technology for the past decade without much financial strain. The position has changed dramatically because of the drop in the oil price (oil probably earned Russia about $8 billion in 1986). It has probably prompted the move towards joint ventures with Western companies to earn foreign exchange for Russia. Russia's gross hard currency debt is at least $35 billion; this could rise considerably by 1990, the level ultimately depending on the oil price and how much the shortfall in foreign exchange can be reduced by higher production and export of gold and diamonds.

Finally, on a more general note, Gorbachev has acknowledged that central planning has become a growing handicap for a complex economy. To maintain the legitimacy of the Soviet system requires some increase over time in per capita real consumption, however modest. Russian citizens are becoming more aware of the growing success of other countries: Japan, the other Pacific Rim countries and now possibly China. This will increase the dissatisfaction felt at all levels of society if the Russian economy continues to be relatively unsuccessful. Gorbachev and other top Politburo members realise this but it is still uncertain whether even he, with all his charisma, vigour and popularity among the population, can in the long run win against the entrenched position of the *nomenklatura* – the top party *apparatchiks* – as well as the inertia of the middle and lower range of the Russian bureaucracy. The previous two times such an initiative was made were Lenin's 'New Economic Policy' in 1921, which temporarily returned large parts of the economy to private hands, and Khrushchev's reforms after Stalin. In the end, both initiatives were overturned.

Nevertheless, Gorbachev is beginning to decentralise the decision-making process in the industrial sector. Under a 'self-financing' scheme, managers and workers in enterprises linked to five industrial ministries will have discretion over most of their profits in that they can invest them, pay out worker bonuses or use them for other ends. On the political side, Gorbachev has called for secret ballots and more than one candidate in the election of regional and local leaders; and for more non-members of the Communist Party to be drawn into influential positions. He has called a nationwide conference in 1987 on broadening democracy in the Soviet Union, the first in 40 years.

Some Sovietologists will argue that he is merely tinkering around the edges and he will not take the system head-on like Deng in China. We feel that Gorbachev could in the end fundamentally change the Soviet system. If he does, there is an unsaturated consumer goods market in the whole of Russia to satisfy for basic products such as cars, TV sets and fridges. He would like to double national income per head by the year 2000. The potential is there to achieve it, but he needs one thing more than anything else – détente.

3. The Global Scenarios and the World Economy

During a week's debate among the 'circle of remarkable men' in late 1985, drawing the strands of the research together, it was decided that two pivotal uncertainties would shape the world system in the 1990s, and the interplay between them would set the broad pattern of the future. The first uncertainty is whether there is going to be a continuing arms race or détente between the US and Russia, and the second whether there is going to be trade conflict between the US and Japan or whether they will resolve their differences in the spirit of accommodation. This latter uncertainty is a crucial aspect of a much wider one, namely the restoration of responsible management to the world economy by co-operation among the leading industrial powers. There are other 'key uncertainties': a Third World War; Aids; the spread of Fundamental Islam; another Middle East War; who is going to get the next hydrogen or atomic bomb. But writing multi-dimensional scenarios based on flexing a large list of 'key uncertainties' confuses everyone and leads to an endless number of scenarios. Our purpose was to provide a simple lens to focus people's attention on scenarios which were interesting from a business perspective.

Let us look at the four possible combinations of the matrix. Firstly, if the US seeks accommodation with Japan but runs a continuing arms race with Russia you have a scenario called 'Imperial Twilight'. It is where the two superpowers diminish in economic significance by the mid-1990s, not through a Third World War, but through the sheer amount of resources required to sustain the arms race. Russia will be virtually bankrupted and America will continue to run a huge budget deficit (and hence trade deficit), which in the longer term denies the country the possibility of sound economic growth. The Japanese would establish an unassailable industrial lead in the world while the US and Russia were 'arming to death'. We feel that this scenario cannot be sustained beyond the mid-1990s because the build-up of stress in the system would have to be released in one form or another. It is

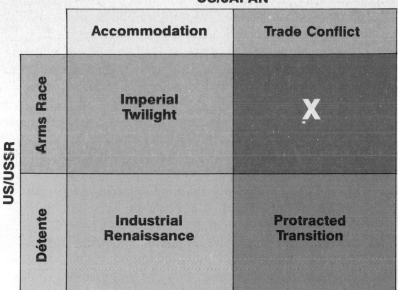

Chart 28 · The 'Key Uncertainties' and the Global Scenarios

a very disappointing scenario of 2 to 3 per cent world economic growth at best – more of the 1980s so far, but certainly not back to the 1950s and 1960s.

We treat as very unlikely the second scenario where the United States takes on both Japan in a trade war and the Russians in an arms race. The US is now too weak to pursue both courses concurrently for any length of time. Equally, the US would be risking its relationship with its other allies since protection is a key strategy of this scenario. Lastly, essential technology from Japan and Western Europe is going to be used in the Star Wars programme, which will be the centrepiece of the next twist in the arms race spiral.

In the third scenario there is détente between the US and Russia, but a trade conflict between the US and Japan. We call this 'Protracted Transition'; it is where the full transition to the new technologies is pushed out into the next century through protection, and in the interim the world economy malfunctions. Trade barriers will be thrown up between the US and Japan, and the rest of the world follows suit with the development of regional trading blocs. The US accommodates Canada and Mexico while Western Europe increasingly trades with Eastern Europe and the African, Caribbean and Pacific countries at the expense of the rest of the world. The Japanese will meanwhile go their own way, developing regional markets including China, and concentrating on exports to other non-Triad countries.

World trade is the flywheel for the growth of the world economy as a whole. In the 1960s world trade grew at 7,5 per cent a year versus world growth of 5 per cent. In 'Protracted Transition', because world trade is restricted to regional zones, world growth is as disappointing as in 'Imperial Twilight' i.e. 2 to 3 per cent a year through to the mid-to-late 1990s. During this period, non-Triad countries suffer – particularly those whose economies are based on natural resource exports – leading to major defaults on debt. In effect the slate is wiped clean as both countries and industries such as agriculture, energy and mining, undergo profound shake-outs. Ultimately, towards the end of the century, the irresistible positive forces of the new technologies make themselves felt, and this factor combined with the ingenuity of world-class companies and reform of the world economic system leads to higher growth by 2005. Not everyone does badly in the early stages of the scenario. Those manufacturing companies with large market shares in protected regional blocs will do well, as will those world-class companies which can vault trade barriers by being insiders in the three legs of the Triad.

One singular feature of 'Protracted Transition' is that it is the scenario in which the Japanese might rearm. It was their cut-off from export markets and the possible cessation of raw material and energy imports that drove them into the Second World War. In this scenario, we could end up eventually with three military superpowers, especially if the US – in addition to closing its markets to Japanese goods – starts withdrawing its military umbrella. The Japanese are at the moment debating the 1 per cent-of-GDP limit on arms: that is significant.

The fourth scenario, 'Industrial Renaissance', is where sense prevails on all sides – in the military dimension between the US and

Russia and in the economic dimension between the US and Japan. Both gates are open. The world is transformed by the new technologies in the 1990s. New industries are spawned on the one hand, and established industries revitalised on the other. We return to the world growth rate of the 1950s and 1960s of 5 per cent a year by the mid-1990s. An early end to the Cold War is combined with a mutually beneficial relationship between America and Japan. The latter may emerge after a sharp confrontation, or more happily through a change in attitudes from both nations to accommodate each other's capabilities and weaknesses. Such a symbiosis would involve a greater economic synchronisation between the US and Japan. Disparities of economic policy – both micro and macro – diminish between the two countries. The American budget and current account deficits are purposefully tackled and reduced; the American savings and investment rates are increased; Japanese capital helps to restructure American industry where Japanese management systems are increasingly incorporated (e.g. participative management). Japan in return opens its markets more substantially to foreign goods, and stimulates internal demand by having a major drive towards improving the quality of life within Japan (e.g. housing). A coherent policy on transfer of knowledge between the two countries and indeed throughout the world is developed, whereby equitable payments for exploitation of others' ideas become obligatory. Invisible income, in the form of royalties, licence income and service fees, becomes an ever more important feature of Triad exports.

In this scenario, both the US and the Soviet Union reduce military expenditure so that the former can concentrate on balancing the budget and the latter on economic reform. The argument has been put forward that reducing the Pentagon budget is deflationary for the US. We would respond that this is quite so in the short term, but it has to be beneficial to growth in the longer term if such a cut will lead to other cuts in, say, welfare entitlements so that the budget deficit is gradually diminished.

In the favourable environment and relatively open trading system which unfold, the non-Triad countries prosper. The international debt problem is slowly eliminated as higher export earnings allow debt repayments to continue as scheduled, while the inflow of new capital into non-Triad countries resumes on a large scale. A concern expressed for this scenario is that Russia, once it has achieved an 'economic miracle' in the 1990s, will be that much stronger and again tempted to dominate the world. We would argue that it is equally likely that economic progress could cause Russia to drop such ambitions as it is drawn into the net of the world economic system. A close monitoring of its foreign policy is the only way of finding out which hypothesis is true.

Although Western Europe is not a main actor in our scenarios, it will not remain passive in the face of events determined elsewhere. The Western European economy will continue to equate to that of the US in size. We think a new realism will appear on the plant floors, and labour markets will become more flexible. The pressures for trade liberalisation within the European community are strong and intensifying, but any progress is contingent upon reform of the Common Agricultural Policy. The importance of a unified market to success in high-tech is increasingly recognised; a European industrial constituency is emerging. These factors are giving renewed momentum to 'negative integration', namely the achievement of a unified market through abolition of internal borders and striving for equivalence of official standards and procedures.

ECONOMIC GROWTH OF THE THREE MAIN ACTORS

The chart on page 79 summarises the inter-relationship between the three main actors. On the horizontal axis we have defence expenditure as a percentage of GNP, and on the vertical axis income per head expressed in constant 1986 dollars.

If you first look at Russia, it is currently estimated to be spending 14 per cent of GNP on arms, while its income is just over $6 000 per head. The orange ray in the diagram denotes the 'Imperial Twilight' scenario. As you can see, the continuation of the arms race compels the Soviet Union to increase its defence expenditure to 18 per cent of GNP in 2005. (We extended this scenario horizon into the next century for the purposes of comparison in this diagram, but as mentioned earlier we believe 'Imperial Twilight' is unstable beyond the mid-1990s.) At the same time the ray is flat, indicating virtually no increase in per capita income. So it is 'all guns for no butter'. Of course if the

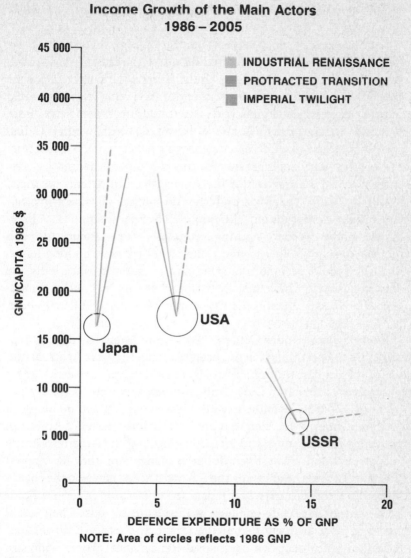

Income Growth of the Main Actors
1986 – 2005

- INDUSTRIAL RENAISSANCE
- PROTRACTED TRANSITION
- IMPERIAL TWILIGHT

GNP/CAPITA 1986 $

Japan

USA

USSR

DEFENCE EXPENDITURE AS % OF GNP

NOTE: Area of circles reflects 1986 GNP

Chart 29 · Income Growth of the Main Actors

Russians can obtain détente and we are in the 'Industrial Renaissance' scenario indicated by the green ray, they can cut back to 12 per cent of the GNP on arms and double their per capita income by 2005.

That is Gorbachev's stated goal in 2000, and it is why he has come up with arms-control proposals every six months. He is in earnest.

The Americans spend only 6,5 per cent of GNP on arms, because their total economy – denoted by the size of the circle – is so much larger than that of the Russians. Under 'Imperial Twilight', US arms expenditure rises to about 7,5 per cent of GNP and, despite stunted growth, there is 'some guns and some butter' as income rises from $17 500 to $26 000 per capita. However, you can see that under 'Industrial Renaissance' the US can cut back to 5 per cent of GNP on arms, balance its budget and raise income to $32 000 per head in 2005. The latter scenario is attractive for the Americans, but détente is crucial for the Russians. That logic underlies the current talks on arms control, but the Americans must be careful. The relevant quote is, "Freedom is another word for nothing left to lose." If the Americans push the Russians into a corner where they feel they have nothing left to lose, they could become frustrated and pursue wholeheartedly the one dimension in which they are a superpower – the military dimension. The Russians could then turn into a hungry and deadly bear, bent on economic prosperity through military domination.

Now to Japan. Under General MacArthur's stewardship, the Japanese did the best thing for themselves, when they put Article 9 into their post-war constitution. That clause (which can be overridden by a two-thirds vote in the Diet) limits military spending to about 1 per cent of GNP. The Japanese have therefore concentrated on being an economic superpower. They have gone from one quarter of American per capita income in 1965 to virtually equalling the American figure in 1986 (and on the latest yen/dollar exchange rate, they have nosed ahead – $18 000 a head versus the $16 000 a head shown on the chart). Under all three scenarios, the Japanese – measured in terms of economic output per head – emerge as the victors in 2005. Their stated goal is to be 20 per cent higher than the US in terms of income per head in the year 2000. In 'Industrial Renaissance' the absolute size of the Japanese economy in 2005 will be approximately equal to that of the US today. Many argue that the Japanese have sacrificed quality of life for their success and in that dimension they lag well behind the US. Nevertheless, they now have the opportunity of trading a small measure of success for an improved quality of life.

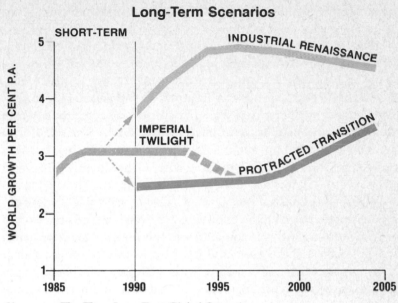

Long-Term Scenarios

SHORT-TERM

INDUSTRIAL RENAISSANCE

IMPERIAL TWILIGHT

PROTRACTED TRANSITION

WORLD GROWTH PER CENT P.A.

5 · 4 · 3 · 2 · 1

1985   1990   1995   2000   2005

Chart 30 · The Three Long Term Global Scenarios

Who would have thought, looking at Japan in the immediate after-math of the Second World War, that it would be so successful by the end of the twentieth century? That is why you do not use forecasts; you look at the world of possibilities. You might have captured Japanese success in a scenario, but never a forecast.

The conclusion derived from the chart is this: the Americans and Russians eye each other as the chief threat, and expensively shadow-box on arms. The Japanese have slipped into the lead. Japan, through sheer competition, has put out of business a large section of America's industrial base. Competition is as lethal as bombs, because those factories have gone for ever. But it is less visible. Hence the military threat of the Soviet Union has figured more highly in the minds of Americans than the economic challenge from Japan.

WORLD ECONOMIC GROWTH

The final global chart indicates the respective growth rates of the world economy for the three scenarios. Under 'Industrial Renaissance' the new technologies push the world up to around 5 per cent

81

growth a year in the mid-1990s. Thereafter the technologies reach saturation level of exploitation and the growth rate gradually declines. It will again pick up after the next burst of innovation in the next century. Under 'Imperial Twilight' and 'Protracted Transition' the world is held in the vice of 2 to 3 per cent economic growth until the mid-1990s. This is tragic for the non-Triad where population growth runs as high as 3,5 to 4 per cent a year. The world may come to its senses after 2000, but one must not underestimate the 'coefficient of irrationality' — it is behind about 50 per cent of world events. In other words, the world is as crazy as it is wise. Consequently, the world could as easily fall into one of the downside scenarios as follow the virtuous path of 'Industrial Renaissance'. That is the whole point of doing the talk and writing the book: it is for decisions and actions, not for academic interest. We should present this material to the principal decision-makers of the world and say, "Look, this is our best shot at the options out there. If you agree with the logic, you should jointly develop strategies to pre-empt the two bad ones and make the good one true. The whole world turns its eyes on you."

For South Africans, it shows what an incredibly tough world it is. There are so many things that South Africa has to do to be a 'winning nation'. Every day spent in limbo, as South Africa is today, is a day lost in the swift global race.

PART II
The South African Scenarios

4. The South African Economy

Turning to South Africa, we start by looking at the South African economy and the way it might develop, before proceeding to essentially political factors and finally to alternative scenarios. First let us put the South African economy into perspective.

SOUTH AFRICA IN PERSPECTIVE

South Africa is an average country with an average economy. Its GDP per capita is about $1 900, which in the world economic rankings puts it with Yugoslavia, Mexico, Malaysia, Portugal, Uruguay, Chile and Brazil – somewhat in the middle of the pack. South Africa's GDP is 1/200th of world GDP – it is tiny, but that is a great asset in South Africa's favour because it can grow fast without threatening anybody. Japan grows fast and it threatens somebody.

As stated in Part One, we are moving into the knowledge-intensive 1990s, where people are going to make more money from knowledge, and less from raw materials. High tech threatens South Africa's commodity exports. If this country did not have its gold, platinum and diamond exports, it would be facing the same current account problems as Australia and other non-Triad countries (putting the external debt issue on one side). However, we ran a rough econometric model at Anglo which showed that, even with the fairly generous assumption that gold production would remain at current levels till the turn of the century, South Africa could face a widening current account deficit from the mid-1990s onwards. That is unless it does something now to create the right environment in which other export industries are developed, such that some of them will turn into major foreign exchange earners by the late 1990s. We assumed a 4,5 per cent a year GDP growth rate from here on. Some might say that figure is too high, but we believe it is needed for a minimum satisfactory growth in real income per capita of 2 per cent, given a population growth rate of 2,4 per cent. A large rise in the gold price in real terms would postpone the moment of truth, but it cannot be counted on nor is it a long-

SOUTH AFRICA IN PERSPECTIVE

* **SA Is an Average Country with Average Economy. GDP/Capita of $1 900 Puts SA with Yugoslavia, Mexico, Malaysia, Portugal, Uruguay, Chile and Brazil**
* **SA's GDP Is $^{1}/_{200}$ of World GDP**
* **Hi Tech Threatens SA's Commodity Exports**
* **SA Has Mid-to-Low Tech Environment. Exception Medicine**

Chart 31 · South Africa in Perspective

term solution. New export industries to fill the gap need to be discovered and grown by current and future generations of entrepreneurs, working as individuals or in teams.

South Africa has a medium- to low-tech environment. It does not possess the education system to support a broad enough high-tech environment to underpin a proper 'first logic' economy and to provide the major impetus for growth in manufactured exports. Medicine, we feel, is an exception in that it approaches Triad standards in many areas and could be a major foreign exchange earner.

Nonetheless, South Africa does have plenty of comparative advantages. The list in the chart below is not exhaustive; it is intended to make people think along the right lines.

SOUTH AFRICA'S COMPARATIVE ADVANTAGES

South Africa has an excellent infrastructure – roads, bridges, electricity grid, etc – from which to launch itself on further growth. The unfortunate thing is that all areas in the country do not enjoy the same quality of infrastructure, but that has to come. South Africa is still number one in the world in important mineral resource categories, including gold. But it is those nations that have no natural resources and therefore have to live off their wits and educate their population who emerge as winners in the global game. South Africa must learn to live off its wits before it runs down on mineral resources.

South Africa has cheapish power. But by world standards South Africa is an energy-intensive economy. It uses 28 per cent more megajoules per unit of GDP than the US.

There is still an important trade route around the Cape. Vital minerals such as coal and iron ore traverse it in bulk carriers, and more of Europe's oil goes round the Cape than through the Suez Canal. The Cape could use its strategic positioning on the world map to turn itself into a 'Cape Kong' one day, and be a major entrepôt like Hong Kong.

South Africa is a beautiful country with a wonderful climate. Our overseas team thought that this country had incredible tourist potential. Last year Spain earned almost as much from tourism – about $7 billion – as South Africa earned from gold. The North-South air route involves no jet-lag for travellers, so under a good political scenario and with good promotion South Africa could become a favourite holiday spot for West Europeans.

The world is moving towards a system of bilateral trade swaps. Countries say to one another, "If you buy one dollar of my goods, I will buy one dollar of yours." South Africa can go to another country and say, "We will buy two dollars of your goods if you will buy one dollar of ours." The reason is that South Africa can pay for that extra

Chart 32 · South Africa's Comparative Advantages

SOUTH AFRICA'S COMPARATIVE ADVANTAGES

✳ **Good Infrastructure**
✳ **Abundant Mineral Resources**
✳ **Cheapish Power**
✳ **Important Trade Route**
✳ **Beautiful Country/Climate**
✳ **Gold Benefit for Bilateral Trade Swops**
✳ **Sophisticated Financial Services**
✳ **Ability to Handle Large Projects**
✳ **Proximity to African Markets**
✳ **Medical Skills**

dollar with the proceeds from gold which is sold anyway through Zürich. South Africa can offer a better than a one-for-one ratio in order to stimulate trade.

South Africa probably has one of the most sophisticated financial services industries, e.g. banking and insurance, in the Southern hemisphere.

Visitors from overseas are astonished at this small nation's ability to handle large projects such as Sasol, Escom collieries and new gold mines; it is part of the tradition of the mining industry to have superb project management skills.

South Africa exports about $750 million worth of goods to countries to the north in Africa. Under a good political scenario South Africa's proximity to Central and Southern African markets is clearly an asset.

Finally South Africa, with its medical skills and favourable climate, can establish an industry to care for the increasing number of elderly people in the Triad who may be looking for a more comfortable place to retire.

THE 'DUAL-LOGIC' ECONOMY

This economic chart is as important as the three political charts I am going to show you combined. No new political dispensation will work unless it is accompanied by a successful economic model. They have

Chart 33 · The 'Dual-logic' Economy

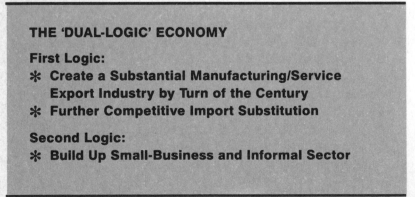

THE 'DUAL-LOGIC' ECONOMY

First Logic:
* Create a Substantial Manufacturing/Service Export Industry by Turn of the Century
* Further Competitive Import Substitution

Second Logic:
* Build Up Small-Business and Informal Sector

to go hand in hand in an integrated strategy. People will judge a new political system not only on its underlying moral fibre, but also on how much extra money it delivers into their pockets (though, as you will see, we will be asking people to take a long-term, not a short-term, view).

South Africa has to develop a 'dual-logic' economy. In the 'first logic' economy, a substantial manufacturing and service export industry must be encouraged to grow alongside the current exporters. Perhaps South Africa should first look at going downstream on mineral exports, and building on existing strengths. Tourism, as we said earlier, is an obvious service export industry. As regards competitive import substitution, we feel there are only limited opportunities to be had there. Most of what is easy to substitute has been substituted. Apart from oil, South Africa's next import substitution challenge is sophisticated machinery.

As mentioned in the global 'rules of the game', 'first logic' companies tend to be giants, which use state-of-the-art technology and capital-intensive processes to compete in the world game. The initial outlays on research and plant can be enormous, which means that the 'first logic' economy can only prosper if its investment requirements can be satisfied. This in turn implies a higher national propensity to save and a return to net capital inflows. For the latter to be achieved, the political situation has to improve. However, the 'first logic' economy will not provide the majority of the jobs. It is in the medium- to small-business and informal sectors that the bulk of the new work-seekers will have to be employed. For this to be so, there has to be a symbiotic relationship between the two economies, where the simpler activities are subcontracted from big to small business. Moreover, medium- and low-tech methods to produce goods and provide services in the 'second logic' economy may well be the most appropriate in order to maximise the number of job opportunities. Lastly, a system of delivering the requisite amount of savings to the 'second logic' economy has to be found, because the 'invisible hand' of the market economy will not work by itself. One of the best ways to kick-start the 'second logic' economy is through embarking on a massive housing programme using small contractors.

It is estimated by the Institute for Futures Research at Stellenbosch that the economically active population in South Africa will be 18 million in 2000, of which between 11 and 15 million will be employed in the formal sector. That leaves a very large number who will need to earn their living in the informal sector. Such a challenge needs a system of government that supports small entrepreneurs and gives them the freedom to flourish.

5. The Background to the Political Scenarios

Having looked at economic considerations, we now turn to essentially political matters before we go on to merge the two into political and economic scenarios.

THE 'RULES OF THE GAME'

We have five 'rules of the game' for the South African political scenarios. The first is the current imbalance of military power in favour of the people in power. We make this the first 'rule of the game' because last year some of the Western media were predicting the downfall of South Africa in a matter of months, rather than in years. However, we rule out any 'instant revolution' scenario. The revolution in the Philippines had two important differences. Firstly, there was one man in power – Marcos – not a significant group as in South Africa. Secondly, the two leading army officers loyal to Marcos, Ramos and Enrile, switched sides. We do not see that action being repeated in South Africa. It is the only action in the short term capable of creating the kind of military balance that would make an instant revolution possible.

The other scenario ruled out by the first 'rule of the game' is 'unconditional surrender': a situation in which the South African government hands over 100 per cent of the power with no guarantees.

Chart 34 · 'Rules of the Game' for the Political Scenarios

'RULES OF THE GAME' FOR SA POLITICAL SCENARIOS

* Imbalance of Military Power
* Equilibrium of Violence
* Industrialised Society
* SA Cannot Fully Satisfy World Agenda
* But Statutory Apartheid Will Go

There is not a single example in the history of mankind where one group has handed over 100 per cent control over its destiny on its own soil to another group when it has held the current military advantage. Examples abound of nations handing over 100 per cent of the power in countries other than their own – that was the decolonisation process. Similarly the Vietnam War was defeat on foreign soil for Americans.

Thus when people talk of negotiating simple transfer of power in South Africa, it is essential that the phrase be defined. If it means unconditional surrender, that is not going to happen in a peaceful fashion. People only surrender unconditionally on their own soil after a fight, when defeat and annihilation stare them in the face.

The second 'rule of the game' is that, no matter how great the military might of those in power, the equilibrium of violence in South Africa will gradually rise under a bad political scenario. A modern society is very vulnerable to urban violence (witness the ongoing violence in Western Europe). As one senior army officer said to me at a talk, "We have a '20-80 rule': 20 per cent of the future can be determined by military means, but 80 per cent has to be resolved by political means." The equilibrium of violence may drop in the short term through application of sheer force, but it can only be minimised on a permanent basis if people generally are satisfied with life.

The first two 'rules of the game' taken together are a recipe for a slowly declining quality of life in South Africa under a status quo: they offer a classic stalemate in the medium term, in which no prospect of military defeat of those in power is balanced against a rising tide of violence.

The third 'rule' is that South Africa is an industrialised society, and in the heart of that society lies the model for the future. For many companies in South Africa life now is very different to what it was in the 1970s. In those days, everything was determined by management. They had the sole prerogative when it came to deciding wages and conditions of service of black workers and everything else affecting workers in the job situation.

The majority of senior management's time was spent on making operating decisions and little time was spent on industrial relations. The annual black wage settlement was concluded in a matter of days by taking the annual rate of inflation and adding a certain percentage. The latter addition occurred for either of two reasons or both: management were aware that the cost of living among black people was rising faster than the average CPI or management wanted to close the wage gap between white and black employees. In short, the future, even with good intentions, was imposed on black employees.

Today where companies are unionised, a large part of senior management's time is spent on industrial relations and in negotiating wages and other issues that affect workers' lives. Of course, the unions will say that not enough is negotiated, but that is part of the negotiation process. What matters is that there are increasingly areas of co-prerogative where the future is negotiated between management and representatives of the workers. It is no longer imposed by one side. Indeed, it would be a delusion not to acknowledge that there is now significant power-sharing in economic terms. The real point, though, is that negotiation works. Rhetoric is dropped, reality prevails and in the end the companies concerned go on producing the minerals, goods and services. There is no turning back in industry; the new order is here to stay.

The industrialised society in South Africa should also be welcomed in another dimension. It provides an opportunity in the workplace for individuals to rub shoulders and communicate with one another for eight hours a day. If you look back to the French and Russian revolutions, there was little if no contact between the aristocrats and the peasants, and all the middle-class bourgeoisie had to do was light a match and drop it. Here you have the daily contact at work between people of all backgrounds, and the imperative of getting on with the job, to pre-empt the same scenario unfolding.

The fourth 'rule of the game' is that South Africa cannot fully satisfy the world agenda – not through peaceful evolution. Several countries are calling for simple transfer of power, and they appear to mean virtually unconditional surrender by the people in power. In a less dramatic sense, other countries are calling for South Africa to deliver the political goods far faster than it is capable of doing. How then can South Africa overcome this 'rule of the game'? The answer is that the country has to work towards a situation where a significant cross-section of South Africans, black, coloured, Asian and white, travel overseas and say, "Stop wrecking South Africa." But the prerequisite is that South Africa is making sufficient progress to give that message. It is no good having a few voices crying in the wilderness and marketing what most people here and overseas acknowledge is a defective product.

And finally statutory apartheid will have to go, because it is being overtaken by the demands of an increasingly integrated and complex economy. People realise it is an ever-greater stumbling-block to being a 'winning nation'. For instance, when education is the prime characteristic of a 'winning nation', the question is more often being posed whether it makes sense to have partially empty white schools, teacher training colleges and technikons. Social values in South Africa are on the whole adjusting too. Witness the gradual opening of beaches, cinemas, restaurants and other facilities to everyone; the growing number of people living in 'wrong' areas according to the Group Areas Act; the fact that there are now no barriers to interracial marriages; and the number of universities and private schools moving towards non-racial admission. Urbanisation is contributing to the change in values. The total urban population in South Africa is said to double from 15 million in 1980 to about 30 million in 2000.

Regarding this 'rule of the game', one professor from an Afrikaans university made an apt comment. He said, "Hendrik Verwoerd had impeccable logic which went something like this: 'If you start down the road on educational and economic advancement for black people, you had better be ready to follow through with social and political advancement. Once you are in the tunnel, you have to come out the other end.' He of course used this to justify digging separate tunnels but, because of the modern economy, all of us are in fact halfway down one large tunnel. That is why the present situation is untenable: excavating a complicated network of separate tunnels is now far too late and costly, and change has to come in a different form."

THE 'KEY UNCERTAINTIES'

Having dealt with the 'rules of the game' for South Africa, we must now examine the 'key uncertainties' facing the country.

We have three 'key uncertainties'. The principal one revolves around the strategies of power of all parties in South Africa. The lat-

94

'KEY UNCERTAINTIES'
FOR SA POLITICAL SCENARIOS

- * **Strategies of Power**
- * **Economic Strategies**
- * **World/SA Dynamic**

Chart 35 · 'Key Uncertainties' for the Political Scenarios

ter can be broadly divided between those who are in power and those who are not. For the people in power, there are two options: either they impose a future on all South Africans, or they negotiate a future with all South Africans. It is a very simple choice. Let us consider the first option. It was probably viable 100 years ago because most people then expected the future to be imposed on them. In Britain in the middle of the nineteenth century, people elected Members of Parliament who were thought to have above-average education and intelligence; the MPs would look after them and make decisions in Parliament on their behalf, whilst the people themselves sat back until the next election. Times have changed. The individual has come to the fore, and a growing number of people around the world want participatory democracy as opposed to representative democracy. They will still elect representatives, but they now want to play an ongoing role in matters directly affecting their own lives as well. In America, power is diminishing at federal level and increasing at state and local level in line with this trend. Power is moving down the system.

Hence, while even fifty years ago the people in power in South Africa could have themselves developed a new constitution which was literally perfect for this country's situation and it would have been accepted, now it would have no chance unless there had been meaningful participation by everybody in the country (or in practice their designated representatives). Everybody now wants to help design the house they are going to live in. In other words, an imposed future will no longer be accepted voluntarily – it can only be implemented through force.

So we must look at the other option: a negotiated future involving all South Africans. But negotiation has to be strictly defined, because frequently the term is used when the process being referred to is consultation. Negotiation means four things to a businessman. Firstly, it always costs you. You have to be prepared for give-and-take. However, it often throws up solutions which no one individually would have thought of and implemented. Faced with a common problem, a group of minds working in combination can be far more creative than any single mind. So negotiation cuts both ways.

Secondly, no one has complete control over the process, because everybody sitting around the table has equal status. No one can unilaterally decide who attends or what the agenda is going to be.

Thirdly, the outcome is uncertain. When negotiating a wage increase, one side may start at 10 per cent and the other side at 40 per cent. No one knows where in the middle the settlement will end up. It is only through the negotiation process that a figure is finally struck.

Fourthly, when you sit down at the table, you want the people sitting opposite to be strong, and in a position to deliver on the agreement eventually negotiated when they report back to their people. In that case, a prerequisite of successful negotiation is that the negotiators have been allowed to establish their credentials – through formal or informal processes – with the people they are representing. They must be perceived to be legitimate representatives.

By contrast, consultation need not cost you; you can always go back to square one because the final decision is in your hands. Secondly, you can control the process, because you have a major say over who is going to come to the table and the agenda. Thirdly, the outcome is uncertain but only on your own terms; you can decide to incorporate other people's ideas if you feel they are better than your own. Fourthly, the strength of the other parties is not central to the process; you are looking for their wisdom, not so much for their ability to deliver on the settlement. So there is a crucial difference between negotiation and consultation. For many companies, consultative committees were merely an interim step to the acceptance of unions which black workers clearly wanted.

Four responses to my talk illustrate the essence of negotiation and the key difference between negotiation and consultation. In the one case, I was asked by a man of considerable political power in South Africa what his options were. I gave him the following choice: "Either you invite the moderate chefs into the kitchen to bake a moderate pie and try and sell that pie to the rest of South Africa; or all the chefs arrange to meet in the kitchen to bake the pie, in which event it may be much easier to sell." His reply was: "Are you saying that I am just another chef?" That is the crux, because in negotiation there are no master chefs. If one were to have the final say over the ingredients of the pie, it would be consultation.

The second striking response came at the Natal Indaba at which I spoke in the middle of July last year. One of the delegates, an Afrikaner, came up to me afterwards and said, "You know, I like what you said about negotiation. I want to tell you what the Indaba has done for me. When I arrived at the Indaba in April, I held my destiny close to my chest. I have now put my destiny on the table as a result of the three months of negotiation. You as an Englishman cannot possibly understand what an incredible shift in outlook it is for me as an Afrikaner to go from there to here." I replied I did because he was actually acknowledging that everybody around the table had equal status and the main objective was to optimise their joint destiny. The process had worked for him and incidentally for most others at the Indaba – negotiation had transformed them as individuals.

The third response came when I was talking to the Uitenhage community – one black shop steward of a large local company got up at the end and said, "What you say about negotiation is true. We have negotiated with our employer and the local community in Uitenhage, and we haven't brought the heavens down. Why, if we can do that, can't we actually be thought responsible enough to negotiate at a national level as well?" Nobody in the audience had an answer for him.

Lastly, this revealing response to the principle of negotiation came from a well-to-do man at one of my talks in Pretoria: "You say negotiation is give-and-take. Tell me, what am I going to take?" My answer was, "Ask your kids – you give nothing; they will lose everything. You take the future."

For the people not in power, there is likewise a twin choice. Either one goes for a winners-take-all pie or one accepts the concept of a common pie in which the size of the slices is to be negotiated. At this point in the talk, I was stopped by a young black man the other day who said, "Before you even start talking about slices of pie, consider these points. We have numbers and youth on our side; after all, there will be 45 million people in South Africa at the turn of the century and only 5,5 million whites. We can only grow stronger. Secondly, we have the world on our side and that is relevant. Finally, it is the world that tells us we have morality and democracy on our side. Hence, the whole pie is there for the taking." So I said, "That means unconditional surrender of whites, so you'll have to fight for it." His reply was, "We accept that. But with South Africa completely isolated, the economy will eventually wind down, and you cannot fight a war with a shattered economy. War will be an easy jive."

Apart from offering to take him to Pietersburg or Brits when I was next talking there to introduce him to some of the people with whom he would be jiving, my response was twofold. First, the only certainty about war is that it is uncertain. When British troops marched into the First World War they thought it would be over in six months. The war lasted four years, and the total combatant death toll was 9,7 million. In the current war between Iran and Iraq, the Iranians thought it would soon be over because of their superior numbers and the Iraqis because of their superior weaponry. Now, six years on, the war has lasted far longer and cost many more lives than either side originally imagined. People go into wars to win and yet there are stalemates all around the world. War is no easy jive.

Second (and more crucially for those who say they have never underestimated the fight on their hands), there is no way, given the global 'rules of the game' and the competitiveness of the world, that the winners-take-all pie at the end of a short or long war can be anything like as large as the common pie with negotiated slices. You cannot fight a civil war and expect to retain your place in the swift global race at the same time. The country has to fall precipitately down the world rankings. In fact, one might even go further and say that a negotiated slice of the common pie could be greater than the entire winners-take-all pie. To this statement, I have been given the reply that Chamberlain was a 'common pie' merchant before the Second World War in terms of his policy of appeasing Germany at any cost to avoid war. Churchill was right to fight. The answer is that the 'common pie' approach requires reasonableness from all principal parties and any one party can render this alternative non-viable by being unreasonable. One veto will mean reciprocal vetoes all round. People may have to fight, and they must be prepared all along to do so. The point of actual commitment, however, ought to be chosen extremely carefully, because the logic of the small winners-take-all pie still stands. To judge the borderline between reasonableness and unreasonableness can be extremely difficult (unlike the case of Hitler). It is so easy to blame your veto on the fact that someone else has given his veto first. The situation can then deteriorate into a finger-pointing exercise in which everybody loses.

I have provided all these illustrations because we are at the crux of the whole future of South Africa. If the choice on the one side were to be an imposed future, the choice on the other would be winners-take-all. If all sides move to genuine negotiation, we think the chemistry of negotiation will work on the people around the table. The number one 'uncertainty' is as simple as that.

The second 'key uncertainty' is concerned with economic strategies. Again, there are two options. Either South Africa moves towards a pragmatic blend of ideologies like the rest of the world, a 'system that works for South Africa' (which we think should be the 'dual-logic' economy), or South Africa is driven by a single ideology which is conceived without resort to the world of experience. In the latter case, we think South Africa will gradually vanish off the world radar screen. When I was pressed recently about where I stood on democratic socialism by a member of a student audience at an English-speaking university, I posed a question in return: "When you use that phrase, do you lay the stress on the word 'democratic' or the word 'socialism'? For me that is critical, because people are sick and tired of having 'isms' laid upon them against their will. Individuals must choose for themselves."

The final 'key uncertainty' is the world/South Africa dynamic: the game played between the world and South Africa. The lynch-pin is sanctions. Now for us the prime issue is: will full-scale sanctions increase or diminish the odds of a negotiated future?

We looked back in history at nations that have been put into quarantine by other countries, and it does not augur well. China was put into quarantine, almost self-imposed, in 1948. It came out of quarantine in 1972, tens of millions of deaths and a few cultural purges later. It certainly did not become more moderate whilst it was in quarantine. In Spain, General Franco was put into quarantine by Europe – he did not become more reasonable. Fidel Castro has not become more amenable to the US by being put into quarantine by it. So, on the whole, once you fully isolate a nation its rulers do not change to suit your wishes; nor do its people become more reasonable to one another – probably they grow less so. We are inclined to think that in this case the future will resemble the past. Hence, the level of sanctions is a 'key uncertainty'.

MODEL OF POLITICAL EVOLUTIONS

In order to write scenarios, you have to build up a model which shows how the system is driven. This chart shows our engine-room. On the vertical axis we have high, low and negative economic growth. On the horizontal axis the section to the left of the red dotted line denotes a situation where the group dominates over the individual; the middle is a transitional period of unknown duration, and on the right you have a state in which the individual matters more than the group.

The first thing to pick out on the chart are the two green stars: these are wished-for states which will never come true. Many people would like to go back to 'Old White South Africa' with a high growth rate. That is not going to happen. If South Africa were to revert to that state it would be isolated, with low-to-negative economic growth. Others would like South Africa eventually to become 'Switzerland', with its canton system: that will not happen either. South Africa could end up in a developed state which is close to Switzerland, and indeed there are commendable principles in the Swiss system which we feel should be applied to South Africa. But in the end South Africa will draw up its own system which works for the people here.

Now for reality. Where is South Africa at the moment? 'Nationalist Power', we feel, sits right on the boundary between the old group-over-individual system and the transitional phase. A crucial assumption of the model is that South Africa cannot go backwards. It will enter the transitional phase. The key is the nature of the alliances to

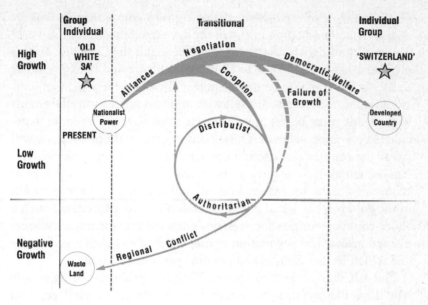

Chart 36 · Political Evolutionary Paths

be forged during transition. They can be forged in two ways – either through negotiation or through co-option. If it is through negotiation, then South Africa could improve its economic growth rate in the medium term to a level which eases the political and social adjustments required for this country to evolve peacefully towards developed-country status. But it is a hard and challenging voyage across the top of the chart, probably without precedent in history. The centrifugal forces, with the potential to rend this country apart, will be strong during the transitional phase. Sacrifices will have to be made on all sides in the short term; but, as one Natal Parks Board ranger put it to me, it is better to be tough and right rather than weak and wrong! In return the 'common pie' could grow at a rate which increases everybody's standard of living in the long run. The growth process itself will lead to a redistribution of opportunities and income, providing one adheres to the principles of the 'dual-logic' economy.

The chart also implies that after the transition South Africa will be non-racial. Individuals will ally with one another on ideas rather than on the basis of groups. Nevertheless, group consciousness will remain as a factor as it does in any of the developed nations of the world (think of the English, the Scots, the Welsh and the Cornish). It is as illegitimate to force people to drop their culture and background as it is to force people into ethnic groups. The degree to which an individual wants to associate himself with or disassociate himself from his background must be left up to him. He must have the freedom to decide. As one approaches developed country status the growth rate will fall as the country can afford a greater degree of democratic welfare. One potential disaster during the transitional process is a failure of economic growth for external or internal reasons, e.g. a major drop in the gold price or a bad global recession or hyper-inflation. Such a shock could precipitate South Africa's descent into the tragic cycle explained below. The negotiation option is full of risk, but it is the only one which leads ultimately to genuine prosperity for all.

The soft alternative is co-option. With co-option you bring people who think like you into the system; you give them the privileges; you redistribute some of the wealth to them. Early on, it looks fine on the surface with the top team taking on an increasingly multiracial complexion. But it is fundamentally flawed, because the social harmony required for consistent growth will not exist underneath. The growth rate will fall as government gets bigger and the work ethic declines. At some point, the right wing cries out, "Enough distribution!" and the country heads back into an authoritarian phase. This in turn leads into another distributist phase when those in power start worrying about the breadth of their support. South Africa goes round and round in the circle in the middle of the chart – each time wrecking the economy that much more.

There is a small possibility of returning to the virtuous option, diminishing with each completed loop. The more likely alternative is for the country to be turned, after one or a few loops, into a military fortress isolated from the rest of the world. It can then descend into a regional conflict and eventually end up in a state we call the 'Waste Land'. Growth will be negative, and some group – we do not know who – will emerge to dominate everybody else. Some people will argue that you have to destroy South Africa in order to rescue it, and cite Germany and Japan as examples. You have to have a total catharsis to purge men's souls. I respond by saying that Germany before the Second World War was relatively far more developed than South Africa is today. It had one of the finest scientific traditions of any nation in the world (particularly in physics). After the war was over it regrouped its considerable 'invisible assets' and, with Marshall Aid of $10,2 billion given to it along with the rest of Europe, it was able to rise like the phoenix from the ashes. Japan likewise was more advanced, and the Korean war gave a great boost to its economy. To say that South Africa, or for that matter, Southern Africa, will repeat that scenario and obtain the required level of aid after a conflict is a perilous assumption. The more likely scenario is a rapid fall in the world economic rankings followed by an extremely long climb back. Any chance of being a 'winning nation' by the turn of the century would be destroyed. It is Vorster's 'alternative too ghastly to contemplate': everyone should contemplate it, because it is only by contemplating it that people will have the reasonableness to embark on the voyage which will safely see this country through the transition.

An interesting question from one politician apropos of the chart was whether you could negotiate and co-opt at the same time. It is not possible because anyone co-opted will immediately lose credibility with his own side, and for that reason would be ruled out of the negotiation process.

6. The South African Political and Economic Scenarios

Having looked at economic factors and the political forces and uncertainties, we now can proceed to develop the political and economic scenarios.

THE POLITICAL SCENARIOS: THE 'HIGH ROAD' AND THE 'LOW ROAD'

We have two basic scenarios for South Africa, arising from the model that has just been discussed, namely, the 'High Road' and the 'Low Road'. The 'Low Road' can degenerate into the 'Cautionary Tale'.

Let us look at the 'High Road' first. The first point is that sanctions have to be kept at a minimal level. In other words, they must not go much beyond the present package. We have asked people overseas what would stop sanctions in their tracks. The almost universal answer, however one may judge it, is, "A sign of a change of process; a tangible indication that South Africa has irrevocably moved to a negotiated future." A frequent response from the audience is that many reforms have taken place, such as the repeal of the Mixed Marriages and Immorality Acts and influx control, but sanctions are still applied. The point is that a new negotiated future is not yet perceived overseas – though in any case many black people will say that the Group Areas Act should just go; one should not wait for negotiation. Another more pungent criticism of the overseas response is the 'shifting goalpost' theory: once you start negotiating, the world will gradually move the baseline so that no concessions are enough short of unconditional surrender of those in power. The answer is that this uncertainty cannot be eliminated. One comes back to the fourth 'rule of the game' that South Africa cannot fully satisfy the world agenda. What has to develop out of the negotiation process is a solid cross-section of people who are willing to put themselves on the line and say, "We're on the 'High Road'. Stop wrecking South Africa."

The second aspect of the 'High Road' scenario is small government (not weak government). The size as well as the composition of government is an issue. The 'High Road' presumes that any future govern-

SOUTH AFRICAN POLITICAL SCENARIOS

High Road:
* Minimal Sanctions
* Small Government
* Decentralised Power
* Joint Negotiation and Synergy

Low Road:
* Increasing Sanctions
* Controlled Economy
* Centralised Government
* Eventual Confrontation and Conflict

Cautionary Tale:
* Fortress South Africa

Chart 37 · The Political Scenarios: The 'High Road' and the 'Low Road'

ment will be the servant of the people and will support them without commandeering them. That is the condition under which a 'dual-logic' economy – particularly the small business and informal sector – will thrive. Power, we feel, will be decentralised for two reasons. It is in tune with the whole trend in the world towards the assertion of the individual; power is moving down in most societies and in many companies. Secondly, once everybody is around the negotiating table, it will become apparent that there are representatives who want a measure of regional and local autonomy. There will be natural checks and balances. How much power is decentralised and how much is retained at the centre is a matter for negotiation. Finally, the centrepiece of the scenario is the process through which it unfolds. We believe it has to be joint negotiation with give-and-take on all sides. Change the process; change the heart. The Indaba example given earlier showed that. If the process is a reasonable one, people will naturally be reasonable with one another and fear will subside. Moreover, the result may well be synergy, whereby the final product is a great deal better than the separate parties to the process originally conceived. Whatever the system of government ultimately developed, it must be acceptable to South Africans as a whole. Genuine democracy in which every single person can participate is the true foe of tyranny.

Under the 'Low Road' scenario, sanctions increase because the future is imposed. The economy becomes more controlled, with import controls, foreign exchange controls, etc. Government becomes more centralised and bigger, just when it should be less centralised and smaller. Co-option superficially works to begin with, but eventually there is confrontation and conflict. The country is locked into the circle of our model, with the possibility of being spun off into a regional conflict. That we call the 'Cautionary Tale' scenario where the country, as stated earlier, turns into a completely isolated military fortress. The dynamic inside the fortress cannot be predicted at all; nobody can say what happens to a nation when you subject it to abnormal stress. But there is no way South Africa can achieve 'winning nation' status under those conditions. The end game, we feel, is the 'Waste Land'. Direct intervention by either military superpower is unlikely whilst the country self-destructs, but cannot be ruled out in the event of potential massacres.

A COMMON VISION FOR SOUTH AFRICANS

You cannot persuade people to take the risk of the 'High Road' by just frightening them with the disastrous consequences of the 'Low Road'. We all talk of the fear of the unknown − never the hope of the unknown − and in the short term the 'Low Road' offers the known path (with comfortable co-option). To launch people into the unknown and make them display exceptional courage − for that is what the 'High Road' entails − requires a common vision. This is our attempt at constructing one.

The most critical part of the vision is to put all South Africans first, plain and simple. 'Being South African' entails looking beyond the categories of colour and groups and realising that individuals are far more complex phenomena with a myriad of associations other than those two. The individual is the basic building-block of mankind; each of us would not possess free will if it were otherwise. The best

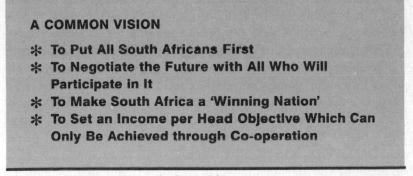

A COMMON VISION

* To Put All South Africans First
* To Negotiate the Future with All Who Will
  Participate in It
* To Make South Africa a 'Winning Nation'
* To Set an Income per Head Objective Which Can
  Only Be Achieved through Co-operation

Chart 38 · A Common Vision for South Africans

analogy as to why South Africans should put each other first is that of a sinking ship with the officers arguing on the bridge. If they go on arguing till the salt water covers their mouths, they all drown. It is in everyone's interest to man the pumps and stop the ship sinking.

The second part of the vision is to negotiate the future with all who will participate in it. The word 'all' should be stressed; we think that there are genuine players from all points of the compass who should be given the opportunity of sitting at the table. We would suggest starting low and aiming high, if one is not to break the crucial condition of equal status around the table. Informal mediation at local, regional and national level could be followed by a SALT*-type process whereby professional negotiators are chosen by all the parties concerned to attend a national forum. The leaders are not directly involved at this point. The forum is where most of the detailed negotiations are conducted, with the representatives reporting back and conferring with their respective leaders. The ground having been carefully prepared, the last stage is where the leaders get around the table to finalise the settlement (the parallel being a summit meeting). To start high with the leaders, when so much is at stake, would be fatal. A SALT-type forum gets the right process on the road and overcomes mistrust without posing insurmountable problems to any side.

Time and again, the response to this aspect of the vision is that the

*SALT stands for the Strategic Arms Limitation Talks conducted between the US and Russia in Switzerland.

other side is totally unwilling to negotiate; it is 'not in their blood' – and that comes from all sides! But negotiation is happening all over the place in South Africa – in local communities, in companies – and the people on either side are no pushovers. It is genuine stuff.

The third part of the vision is to make South Africa a 'winning nation'. This means going through the checklist given in Part One point by point, and developing a long-term integrated strategy. In this context, it is as well to say that no small- or even medium-sized nation has for any length of time gone against the global 'rules of the game' and emerged a winner. Whilst retaining your sovereignty, you have to abide by the logic of the world economy (many members of the non-Triad and even the two superpowers – America and Russia – have now realised that).

The fourth part of the vision is to set an income-per-head objective which can only be achieved by co-operation. The target should be set for say the year 2000. It must offer a real challenge, no group being able to achieve it by pursuing their own interests to the exclusion of all others; it can only be met by all South Africans working together as individuals. Japan set such an objective in 1960 – it was to double national income by 1970. They did it. Now their objective is to be 20 per cent ahead of the US in terms of income per head by the year 2000. They will almost certainly attain that too. To give you an example of what this objective rules out, several people have indicated to me that their 'High Road' is my 'Low Road', and their 'Low Road' is my 'High Road'. To which my response is that the objective gives them a clear choice. They can either be poor and selfish or be rich and sharing; the one thing they cannot be is rich and selfish at the same time.

To illustrate how important a vision is for a nation, we can look at Brazil, which is experiencing very tough times. Here is a recent quote from the Brazilian President José Sarney: "No one should expect Brazil with its riches, with its potential, with its determination, to be a second-rate country; we have a different vision of ourselves." South Africans too should have a different vision of themselves. As I said at the very beginning of this book, the scenario process is about the 'active future' which you make happen, not the 'passive future' which you let happen to you. Alas, so many people during question time at my talks have offered historical reasons and modern-day analogies to support the argument that South Africa cannot take the 'High Road'. In answer I always ask, "What is the alternative?"

ECONOMIC GROWTH ON THE 'HIGH ROAD' AND THE 'LOW ROAD'

The final chart was taken from an earlier Anglo exercise, when we employed one of Western Europe's leading political-risk analysts to do a survey of South Africa for us. Incidentally, he wrote the 'fortress' scenario. One of the conclusions of the exercise was that South Africans grossly underestimated their potential. Under a 'High Road' scenario, South Africa could experience not the Triad's idea of high growth of 5 per cent a year, but 10 per cent a year like some of the smaller Pacific Rim countries. Eventually the growth rate would diminish as the economy grew larger.

Two reasons backed this conclusion. South Africa has an intensity of talent and vibrancy among all its people which is unmatched in the rest of Africa, and to which several European nations cannot hold a candle. Secondly, on the 'High Road' the Triad will invest large sums in South Africa because it is the gateway through which the whole of Southern Africa and parts of Central Africa can be developed. I tested the latter hypothesis on some West European and Japanese businessmen, who confirmed that South Africa was a major investment opportunity under a good political scenario.

Another conclusion, as the chart shows, was that 'Low Road' growth in the short term could be better than the 'High Road'. The 'Low Road' offers import substitution, cheap acquisition of foreign assets and orderly co-option. If in addition the gold price goes to $600, everybody will think they are on the 'High Road'. But it is a complete trap; there has not been the fundamental change of process vital to be properly on the 'High Road'. Eventually, the 'Low Road' crosses the 'High Road' as the cracks in the economy appear, and growth drops to a level where per capita income declines in real terms. (The exact date of intersection of the two lines cannot be predicted. The history of South Africa is strewn with ill-judged predictions. In this case, the lines in the diagram are freely drawn.) Once in the circle of our model or in a regional conflict, overall growth can go negative. An essential implication of this chart is that while South Africa can

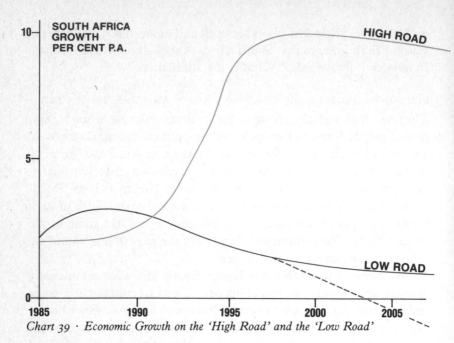

Chart 39 · *Economic Growth on the 'High Road' and the 'Low Road'*

oscillate between the 'High Road' and 'Low Road' paths in the short term, once the lines cross the odds will gradually diminish of jumping from the 'Low Road' to the 'High Road'. Ultimately, there will be no middle ground. At one talk a woman said to me, "Men only learn through experience; they have to go through the 'vale of tears'. Hence the 'High Road' should have a drop in the short term to administer the requisite shock." I replied, "Perhaps. But if the 'vale' is too long, it ends in permanent misery." When I give the talk to young people at secondary school and university, this chart has a profound effect on them. They are the ones who are suffering and will suffer in the 'vale'. They are also the ones who will be hitting their prime when the options start diminishing and the middle space starts going blank.

A member of another audience asked a memorable question: "I hear you're producing a video. Tell me, when I go to the video shop, will I find it under humour or tragedy?" The choice is there. However, we do not think politicians alone should be examining how to get on the 'High Road' in South Africa; everybody should do so within their own universe. Businessmen should ask how they can make their companies walk tall on the 'High Road' in the 1990s. How can one evolve a management structure which truly reflects South Africa and harmonises with the society of the 'High Road'? How can one create a feeling of psychological ownership of the company among all workers? How can one make the management process more participative in line with the trend in individual values? How can one help outside the factory or office so that individuals work more effectively as a team? These are profound questions, which it is not up to this book to answer.

My parting shot is this. Just think that 200 years ago, in the summer of 1787, there was a nation which was in danger of falling apart. Then fifty-five men assembled at a convention and drew up a document which has served as the basis of government for that nation ever since (with 26 amendments). The place was Philadelphia and the nation was America. That event was not predictable – it was made to happen by great men. The same can be made to happen here. I hope that this book has sown the seeds of action, because in the end it is only action that counts.